First Steps: Developing BizTalk Applications

ROBERT J. LOFTIN

firstPress™

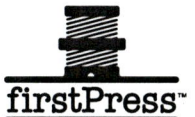

First Steps: Developing BizTalk Applications

Copyright © 2007 by Robert Loftin

All rights reserved. No part of this work may be reproduced or transmitted in any form or by any means, electronic or mechanical, including photocopying, recording, or by any information storage or retrieval system, without the prior written permission of the copyright owner and the publisher.

ISBN-13 (pbk): 978-1-59059-849-8

ISBN-10 (pbk): 1-59059-849-0

Printed and bound in the United States of America (POD)

Trademarked names may appear in this book. Rather than use a trademark symbol with every occurrence of a trademarked name, we use the names only in an editorial fashion and to the benefit of the trademark owner, with no intention of infringement of the trademark.

Lead Editor: Jonathan Hassell

Technical Reviewer: Stephen Kaufman

Editorial Board: Steve Anglin, Ewan Buckingham, Gary Cornell, Jason Gilmore, Jonathan Gennick, Jonathan Hassell, James Huddleston, Chris Mills, Matthew Moodie, Dominic Shakeshaft, Jim Sumser, Matt Wade
Project Manager: Tracy Brown Collins

Copy Edit Manager: Nicole Flores

Assistant Production Director: Kari Brooks-Copony

Compositor: Richard Ables

Cover Designer: Kurt Krames

Manufacturing Director: Tom Debolski

Distributed to the book trade worldwide by Springer-Verlag New York, Inc., 233 Spring Street, 6th Floor, New York, NY 10013. Phone 1-800-SPRINGER, fax 201-348-4505, e-mail `orders-ny@springer-sbm.com`, or visit `http://www.springeronline.com`.

For information on translations, please contact Apress directly at 2560 Ninth Street, Suite 219, Berkeley, CA 94710. Phone 510-549-5930, fax 510-549-5939, e-mail `info@apress.com`, or visit `http://www.apress.com`.

The information in this book is distributed on an "as is" basis, without warranty. Although every precaution has been taken in the preparation of this work, neither the author(s) nor Apress shall have any liability to any person or entity with respect to any loss or damage caused or alleged to be caused directly or indirectly by the information contained in this work.

The source code for this book is available to readers at `http://www.apress.com` in the Source Code/Download section.

Contents

About the Author... v
Introduction vii

PHASE 1   Creating, Deploying, and Testing a BizTalk Application 1

                     Visual Studio 2005 Tasks 1
                           Create the BizTalk Project 1
                           Add an Orchestration.. 2
                           Add a Message to the Project 4
                           Add a Port Type 5
                           Add Ports to the Orchestration 7
                           Add Receive and Send Shapes to the Orchestration............. 9
                           Assign a Strong Name to the Assembly 11
                           Assign the Project a Name................................... 13
                           Build and Deploy the Project 13
                     BizTalk Server Administration Console Tasks 13
                           Launch the BizTalk Server Administration Console 13
                           Add and Configure a Receive Port and a Receive Location 14
                           Add and Configure a Send Port 21
                           Configure the Application................................... 25
                           Launch and Test the Application.............................. 27
                     Summary.. 27

PHASE 2   Working with Schemas 29

                     Visual Studio 2005 Tasks 30
                           Add a Schema to the Project 30
                           Generate an Instance Document 35
                           Validate the Instance Document.............................. 36
                           Force a Validation Failure.................................... 38
                           Promote a Node.. 40
                           Assign the Schema to a Message 41
                           Use the Message in the Orchestration 44
                           Add and Configure a Decide Shape 44
                           Add and Configure a Terminate Shape........................ 47
                           Deploy the Project 49
                     BizTalk Server Administration Console Tasks 49

Launch the BizTalk Server Administration Console 49
Review the Receive Location and Send Port Configurations 49
Change the Receive Location Pipeline 50
Test Your Application 50
Use the Health and Activity Tracking Tool 51
Summary. 57

PHASE 3   Message Mapping. 59

Visual Studio 2005 Tasks 59
Add a Flat-File Schema to the Project 59
Map Fields from the Input Message to the New Message. 62
Validate the Map 64
Test the Map 66
Modify the Orchestration 66
Add a Transform Shape 67
Add a New Port Type and a New Port. 70
Add a Send Shape. 71
Add a Send Pipeline. 72
Deploy the Project 74
BizTalk Server Administration Console Tasks 75
Launch the BizTalk Server Administration Console 75
Review the Receive Location and Send Port Configurations 75
Add and Configure a Send Port 76
Configure the Application. 79
Launch and Test the Application. 81
Sending E-mail from a BizTalk Orchestration 82
Reconfigure the Send Port 83
Configure the SMTP Adapter 85
Summary. 89

About the Author

ROBERT LOFTIN has extensive experience as a development manager, project leader, application architect, and senior Visual Basic .NET developer, who has been involved in managing, designing and developing projects on multiple hardware and operating system platforms and for all software development life cycle phases. He has experience in .NET, web, client/server, imaging, and OOD technologies.

Introduction

When I first decided to learn about BizTalk, I went to Microsoft's site and downloaded the 120-day evaluation copy along with all of the available documentation and tutorials. I worked my way through one of the tutorials, and I then purchased a book about BizTalk. Even though the book and the Microsoft documentation were helpful, I still did not feel comfortable with my level of understanding of the product. The problem I had with those materials is that they were reference works written by experts who I think forgot what it was like to learn a new, complicated subject. Also, it seemed as if the tutorials were designed to show off the capabilities of the product rather than serve as a learning aid.

As part of my education, I decided to create and test my own simple application and keep notes as I went, because I wasn't sure when I would get to use BizTalk for a client. The notes were to be a refresher when called upon by a client to use BizTalk. Those notes morphed into this book.

Note ➡ The information in this book is intended to help you to quickly become familiar with the tools necessary to create, deploy, configure, and launch a BizTalk application. *It is not intended to be a comprehensive BizTalk reference.* Extensive reference information about developing BizTalk applications can be found at Microsoft's site: http://www.microsoft.com/biztalk.

Methodology

The underlying principle of this book is that you learn by doing. Therefore, you will start by creating, deploying, configuring, launching, and testing a simple application. You will then progressively enhance, redeploy, reconfigure, launch, and test the same application in a phased approach (the following illustration shows the finished application). This approach should be very familiar to most developers, because we frequently use a phased approach to deliver software products.

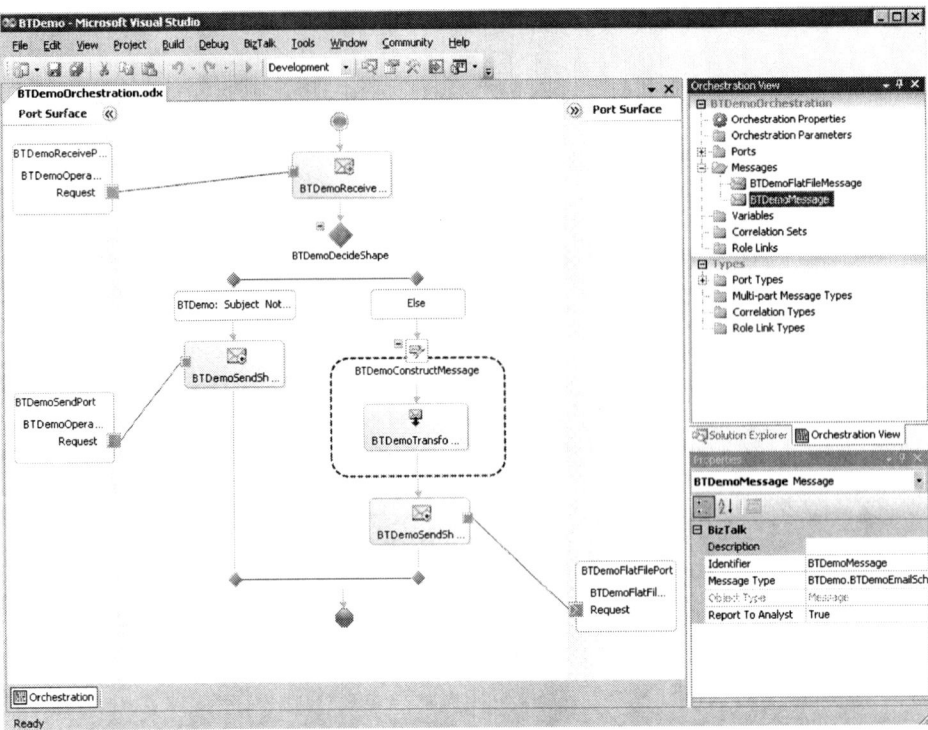

My aim is that by the time you finish this book I will have addressed most of the important features of the tools to such an extent that you will be comfortable enough to venture off on your own.

Note ➡ Because the material in this book is presented using a phased approach, it is critical that you perform the tasks in the order in which they are presented. *Do not jump ahead*. If the results you get are different from the results specified herein, retrace your steps and repeat the tasks until your results match the results specified within this book. Screenshots are used extensively to keep you oriented and show you the results that you should be getting.

Intended Audience

This book is intended for developers who have little or no experience with BizTalk. However, I assume that readers of this book will have at least read some of the promotional materials and white papers about the product on Microsoft's web site.

Required Software and Setup

Completion of the tasks within this book require the following tools:

- BizTalk Server 2006 with a compatible version of SQL Server
- Visual Studio 2005 with BizTalk templates
- .NET Framework SDK

This book assumes the following about your setup:

- BizTalk has been properly installed and connected to the SQL Server database.
- Visual Studio 2005 has been installed on the same computer as BizTalk Server 2006, which makes the BizTalk templates and other BizTalk-related functionality available within Visual Studio 2005.
- The utility for creating strong name key files (sn.exe) that is included with the .NET Framework SDK is available.
- You have administrator rights on the machine that hosts the BizTalk server.

PHASE 1

Creating, Deploying, and Testing a BizTalk Application

In this phase of the project, you will create, deploy, and test a BizTalk application that will copy an XML message from one port to another. To do so, you will use Visual Studio 2005, the .NET Framework SDK, and the BizTalk Server 2006 Administration console, respectively.

You will use Visual Studio 2005 to design and build your BizTalk application, and the BizTalk Server Administration console to install, configure, launch, and troubleshoot the application. The tasks that must be performed in each tool appear in their own sections to assist you in knowing when to transfer from one tool to the other.

Note ➡ This phase takes approximately one hour to complete.

Visual Studio 2005 Tasks

The tasks that you will perform using Visual Studio 2005 are covered in detail in the sections that follow.

Create the BizTalk Project

There are several files that, when used together, compose a BizTalk application. You will use Visual Studio 2005 to create those files. Jointly, those files are thought of as a BizTalk project.

1. Launch Visual Studio 2005.
2. Select File ➤ New ➤ Project menu. Your screen should resemble Figure 1-1.

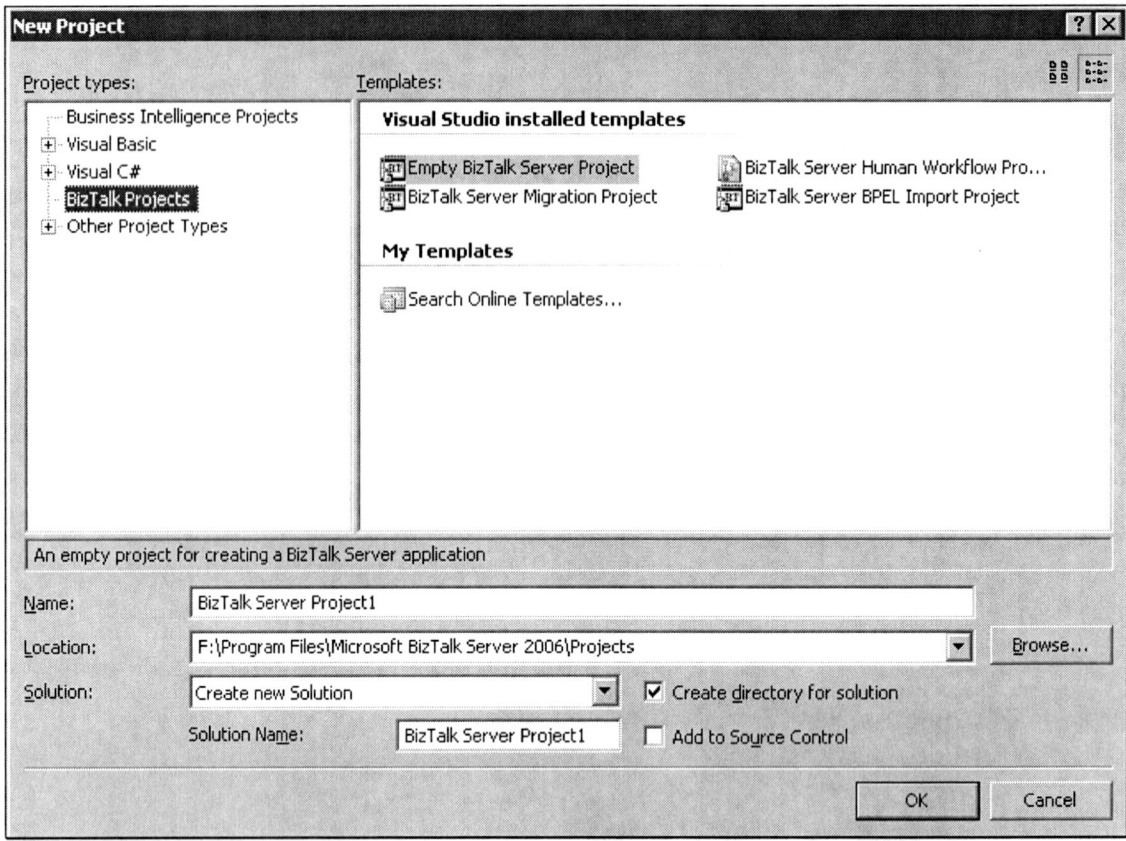

Figure 1-1. Creating a new BizTalk project with the BizTalk Server Project template

3. Enter the name of the project that you are going to create (**BTDemo**, for this example) and click the OK button.

Add an Orchestration

Orchestration is BizTalk-speak for a program. It is the way that you use logic to implement business functionality. When creating an orchestration, you don't use a programming language such as Visual Basic .NET or C#. Instead, you program using objects, as shown in the following steps.

1. Add an orchestration to the BTDemo project by right-clicking the BTDemo project in Solution Explorer and selecting Add ➤ New Item. Your screen should resemble Figure 1-2.

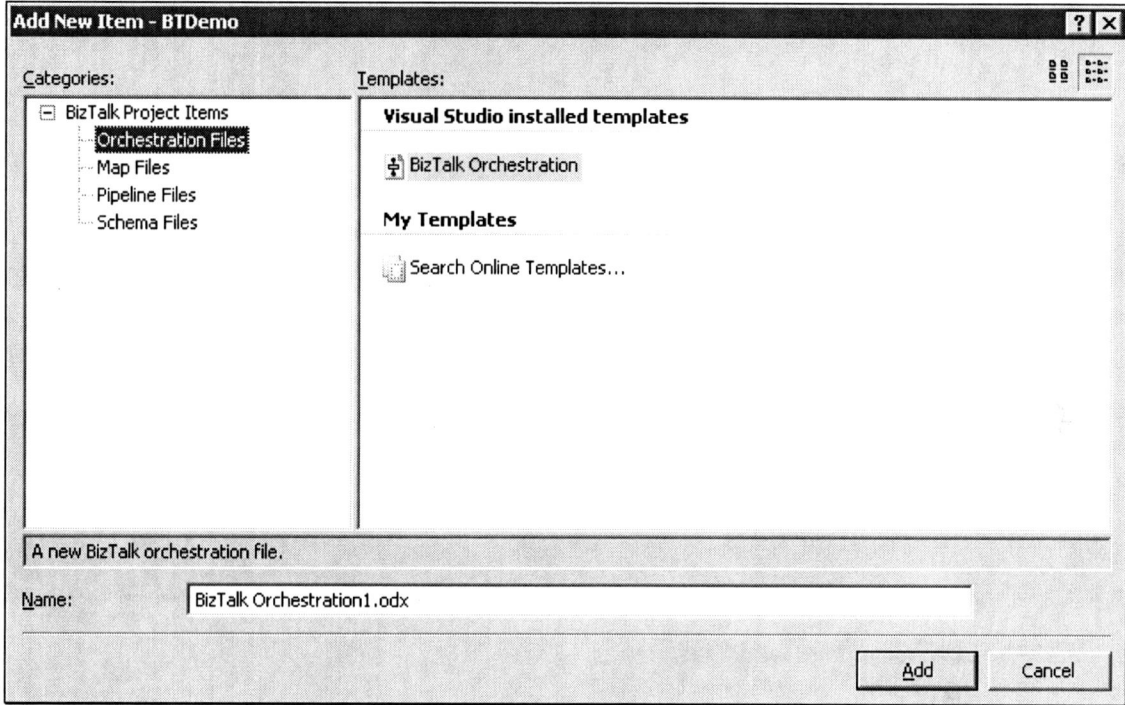

Figure 1-2. Creating a new orchestration

2. Change the name of the orchestration to **BTDemoOrchestration.odx** and click the Add button. Your screen should now look like Figure 1-3.

4 *firstPress: Creating, Deploying, and Testing a BizTalk Application*

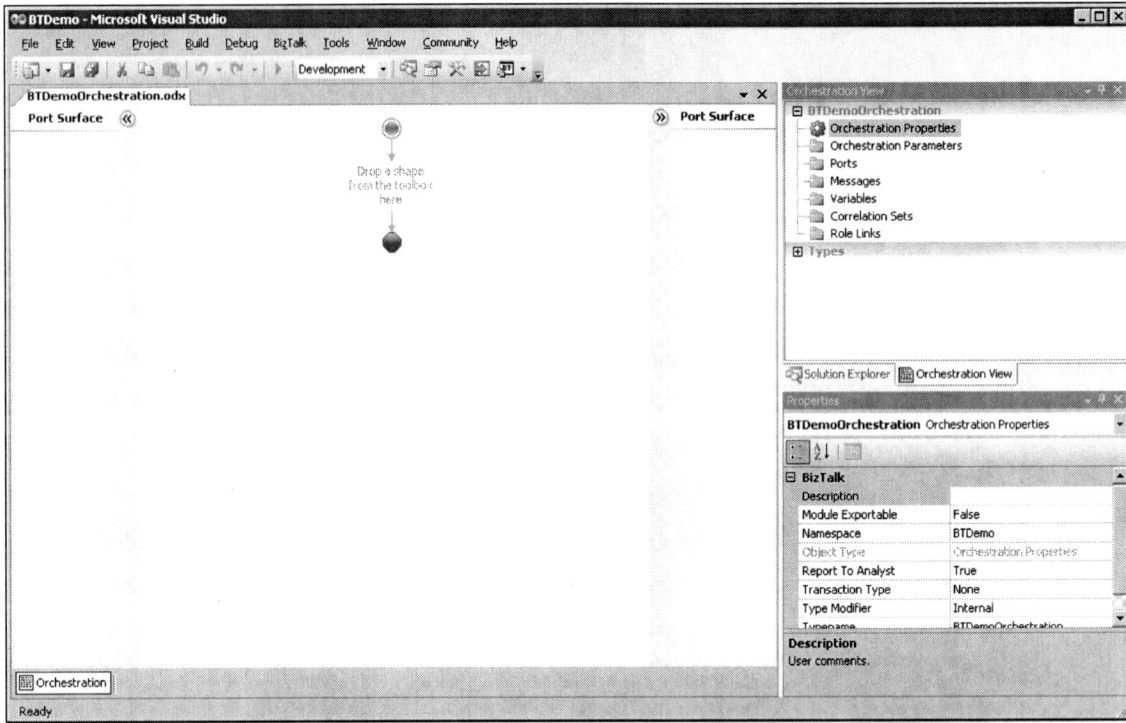

Figure 1-3. Orchestration Design Surface

Add a Message to the Project

BizTalk communicates with other systems via *messages*. Messages may be in an XML or flat-file format. To create a message, follow these steps:

1. Click the Orchestration View tab in Solution Explorer and add a new message by right-clicking the Messages folder and selecting the New Message menu option. Your screen will resemble Figure 1-4.

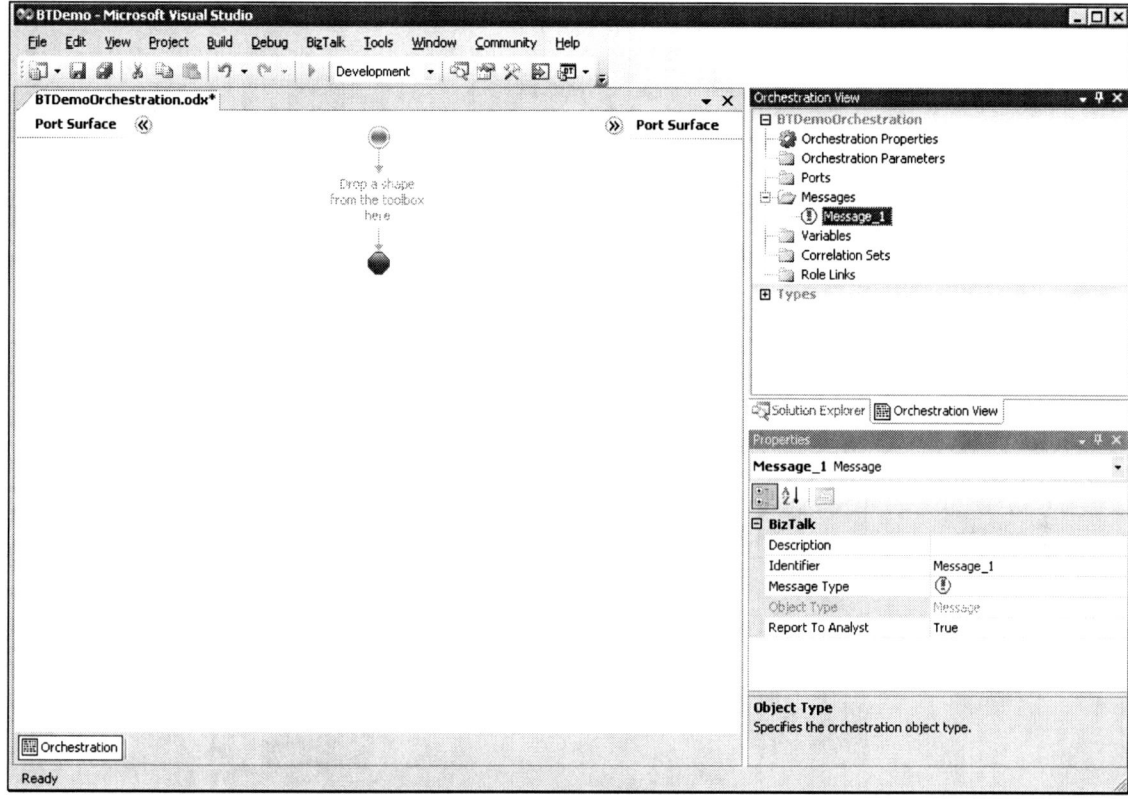

Figure 1-4. Adding a message

2. In the Properties window, configure the Message_1 message as follows:

Property	Value
Identifier	BTDemoMessage
Message Type	.Net Classes ➤ System.Xml.XMLDocument

Add a Port Type

Messages arrive into BizTalk or are sent from BizTalk via *ports*. Ports must be configured to handle different types of messages (e.g., XML, flat file, etc.). A *port type* is used to identify the type of message(s) a port will be handling. To add a port type, follow these steps:

1. Expand the Types node in Orchestration View to display the Port Types folder. Right-click the Port Types folder and select the New One-way Port Type menu option. Your screen should resemble Figure 1-5.

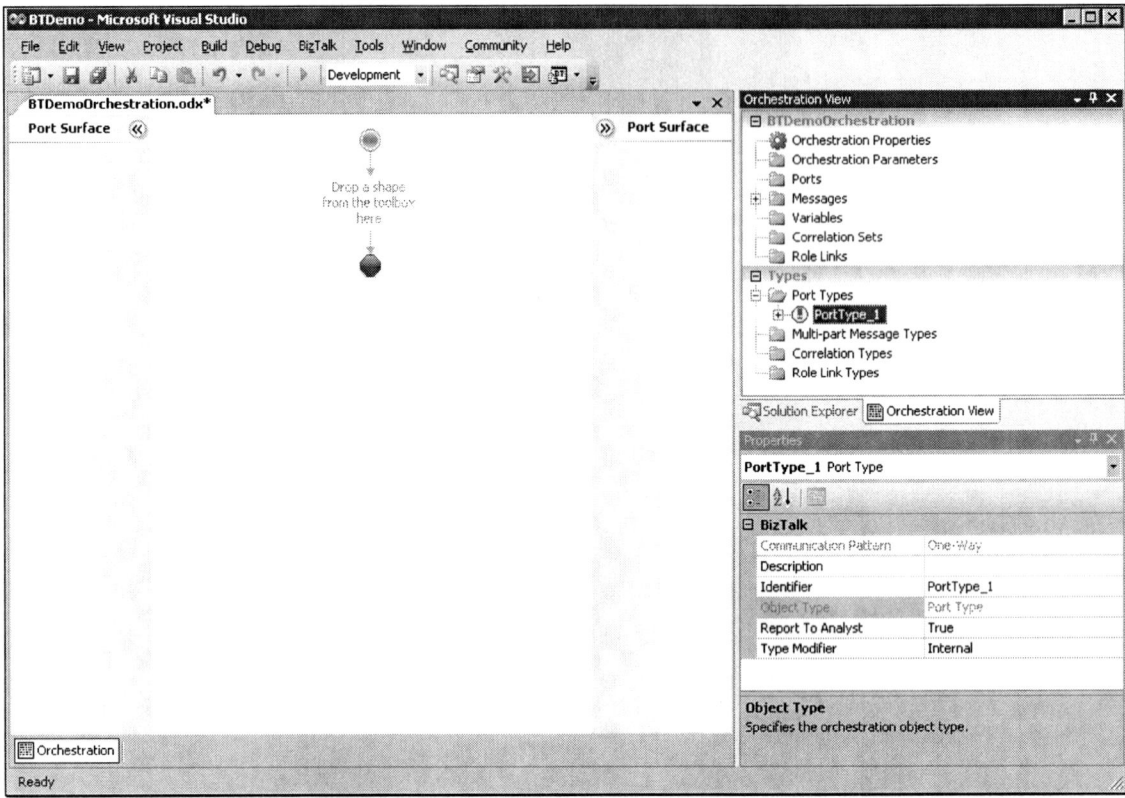

Figure 1-5. Adding a port type

2. Expand the PortType_1 node and configure it as follows:

Property	Value
Port Type ➤ Identifier	BTDemoPortType
Operation ➤ Identifier	BTDemoOperation
Operation Message ➤ Message Type	.Net Classes ➤ System.Xml.XMLDocument

Note ➡ The Message Type property is used to specify the structure or format of the message that will be processed by the port. In the preceding example, you are informing BizTalk that any message arriving at a port using this port type will be a System.XML.XMLDocument. Messages arriving at the port that aren't a System.XML.XMLDocument will not be processed correctly.

Add Ports to the Orchestration

To add ports to the orchestration, follow these steps:

1. Display the Toolbox by selecting View ➤ Toolbox.
2. Drag a Port shape from the Toolbox onto the Port Surface, which launches the Port Configuration Wizard. When prompted by the wizard, enter the following information:

Property	Value
Name	BTDemoReceivePort
Use an Existing Port Type	Selected (Note: Select BTDemo.BTDemoPortType.)
Port Direction	I will always be receiving messages on this port.
Port Binding	Specify later

Note ➡ Although it is possible to specify port bindings at design time, specifying them when you configure the application on the BizTalk Server provides the option of changing the port's settings if/when the needs of the application change, without you having to recompile and redeploy them.

3. Drag another Port shape from the Toolbox onto the Port Surface to launch the Port Configuration Wizard. When prompted by the wizard, enter the following information:

8   *firstPress: Creating, Deploying, and Testing a BizTalk Application*

Property	Value
Name	BTDemoSendPort
Use an Existing Port Type	Selected (Note: Select BTDemo.BTDemoPortType.)
Port Direction	I will always be sending messages on this port.
Port Binding	Specify later

4. Once you have added the ports to the Orchestration Design Surface, your screen should resemble Figure 1-6.

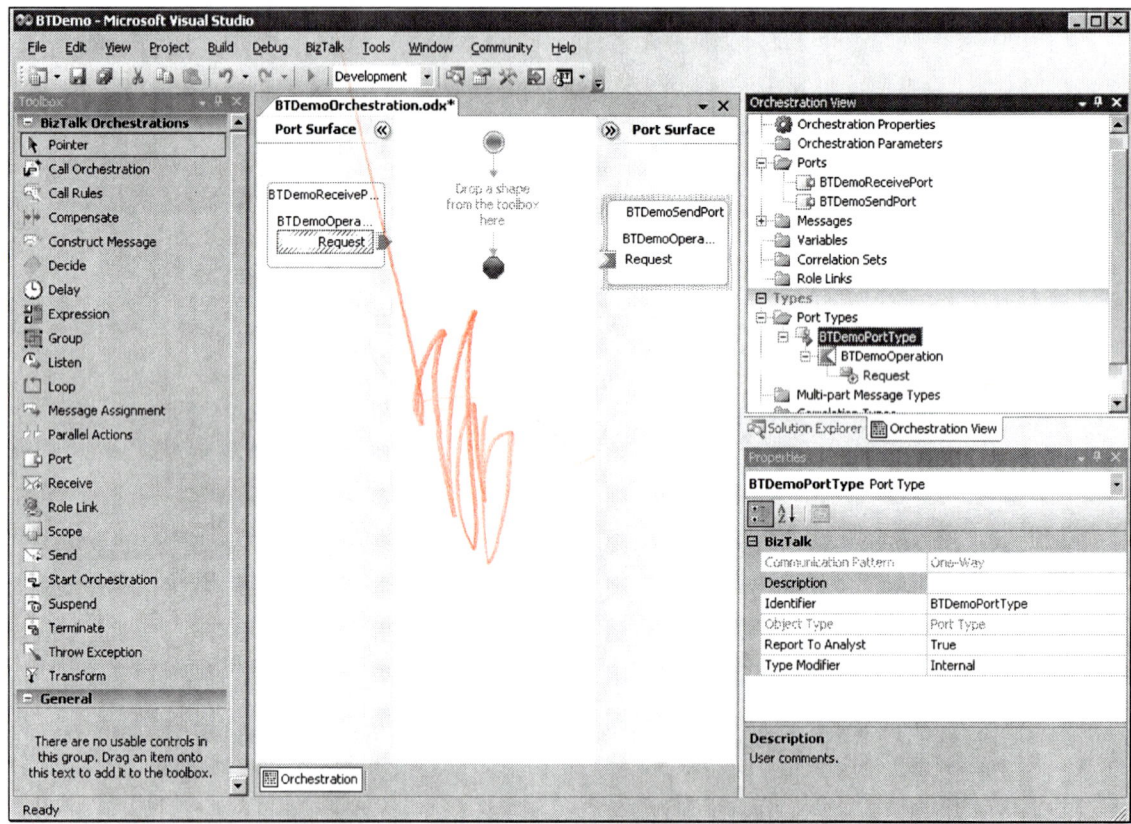

Figure 1-6. Adding ports to an orchestration

Note ➡ It doesn't matter which Port Surface your ports appear on. However, it is common practice to place ports that receive messages on the left and ports that send messages on the right.

Add Receive and Send Shapes to the Orchestration

Receive and Send shapes are BizTalk objects that an orchestration uses to communicate with Receive and Send ports, respectively. Here's how to add them to our orchestration:

1. Drag the Receive shape onto the Orchestration Design Surface at the point labeled "Drop a shape from the toolbox here."

2. Drag the Send shape onto the Design Surface beneath the Receive shape. Your screen should resemble Figure 1-7.

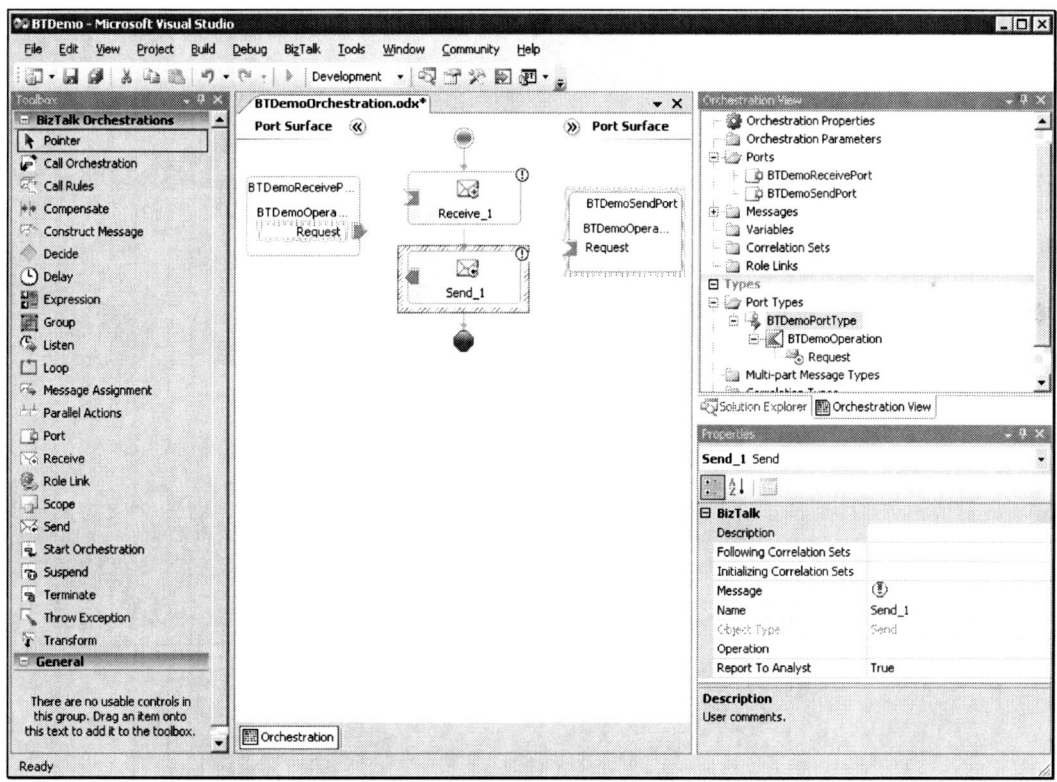

Figure 1-7. Adding shapes to the orchestration

3. Configure the Receive shape as follows:

Property	Value
Activate	True
Message	BTDemoMessage
Name	BTDemoReceiveShape
Operation	BTDemoReceivePort.BTDemoOperation.Request

Note ➡ The Activate property of the first shape in the orchestration must be set to True. If the Activate property is set to False, the orchestration must be called by another orchestration in order to run. Because this is the only orchestration in our project, Activate must be set to True. Failing to set this property to True will result in the following error when you attempt to build the application: "You must specify at least one already-initialized correlation set for a non-activation receive that is on a non-self-correlating port."

4. Configure the Send shape as follows:

Property	Value
Message	BTDemoMessage
Name	BTDemoSendShape
Operation	BTDemoSendPort.BTDemoOperation.Request

5. Your screen should resemble Figure 1-8.

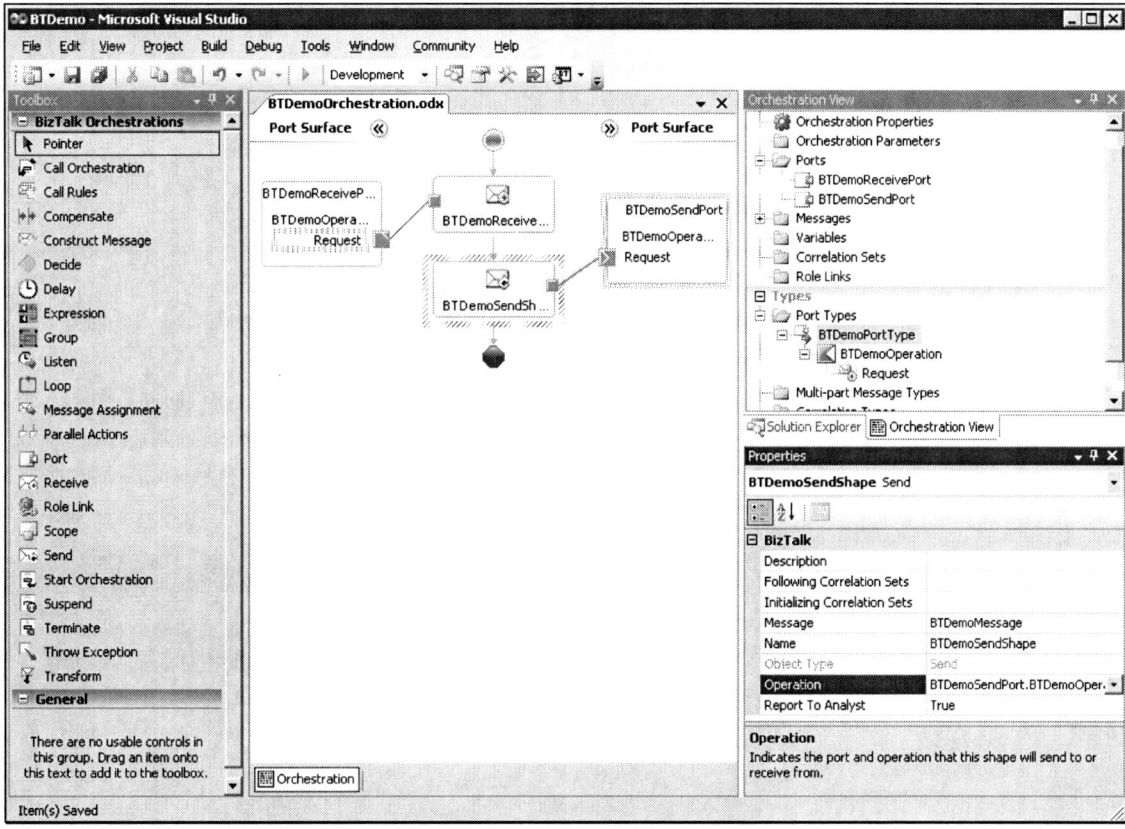

Figure 1-8. Orchestration with configured Receive and Send shapes

Assign a Strong Name to the Assembly

BizTalk projects are .NET assemblies, and they are deployed into the global assembly cache (GAC). However, before an assembly can be added to the GAC, it must have a *strong name*.

Strong names help the .NET Framework uniquely identify assemblies in the GAC. Strong names require a strong name key. The strong name key is generated by the sn.exe tool, which is part of the .NET Framework SDK.

12   *firstPress: Creating, Deploying, and Testing a BizTalk Application*

Note ➡ More information about generating strong name key files can be found at http://msdn.microsoft.com/library/default.asp?url=/library/en-us/cptools/html/cpgrfstrongnameutilitysnexe.asp.

Caution   Before you proceed any further, you must generate a strong name key file.

1. Open the BTDemo Property Pages dialog box for the project by selecting the Project ➤ BTDemo Properties menu option.
2. Select the Common Properties ➤ Assembly node in the left pane and, in the right pane, scroll down to the Assembly Key File property and enter the name of a key file to be used for assigning a strong name to the assembly. Your screen should resemble Figure 1-9.

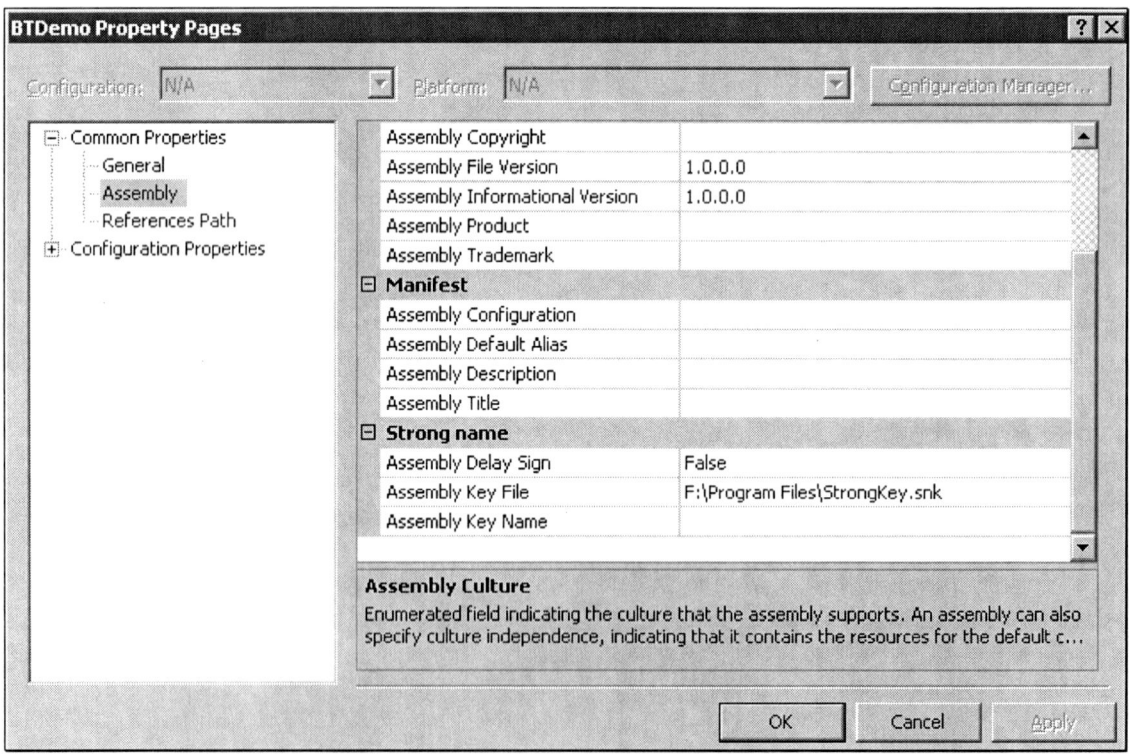

Figure 1-9. Assigning a strong name to an assembly

Loftin

Assign the Project a Name

Assign the project a name by selecting the Configuration Properties ➤ Deployment node in the left pane. In the right pane, enter **BTDemo** as the Application Name. Click the OK button to close the Property Pages dialog box.

Note ➡ If you don't assign the project a name, the project's artifacts will appear under the default BizTalk application on the BizTalk server: BizTalk Application 1.

Build and Deploy the Project

Follow these steps to build and deploy the project:

1. Select Build ➤ Build BTDemo. You should get the message Build Succeeded at the bottom of the Visual Studio window.

2. Select Build ➤ Deploy BTDemo. You should get the message Deploy Succeeded at the bottom of the Visual Studio window.

3. Save the project and close Visual Studio.

BizTalk Server Administration Console Tasks

The tasks that you will perform using the BizTalk Server Administration console are detailed in the sections that follow.

Launch the BizTalk Server Administration Console

You use the BizTalk Server Administration console to install, configure, launch, and troubleshoot your BizTalk application.

1. Launch the BizTalk Server Administration console.

2. Refresh the BizTalk Group by right-clicking the BizTalk Server 2006 Administration ➤ BizTalk Group ➤ Applications ➤ BTDemo node and selecting the Refresh menu option.

3. Expand the BizTalk Server 2006 Administration ➤ BizTalk Group ➤ Applications ➤ BTDemo node.

Add and Configure a Receive Port and a Receive Location

When you created the orchestration in Visual Studio, you deferred the specification of the port bindings. You will now use the BizTalk Server Administration console to specify those bindings. By using the BizTalk Server Administration console to specify the bindings, you have the flexibility to *change* the source of the incoming message(s) as the needs of the application change, without having to recompile and redeploy the BizTalk application.

A *receive location* represents the source of a message. It could be a file, an MSMQ queue, a SOAP URL, and so forth. Receive ports can have multiple receive locations, which allow you to simultaneously receive messages from multiple locations into the same receive port.

To add and configure a receive port and a receive location, follow these steps:

1. Add a receive port by right-clicking the Receive Ports folder and selecting the New ➤ One-way Receive Port menu option. Your screen should resemble Figure 1-10.

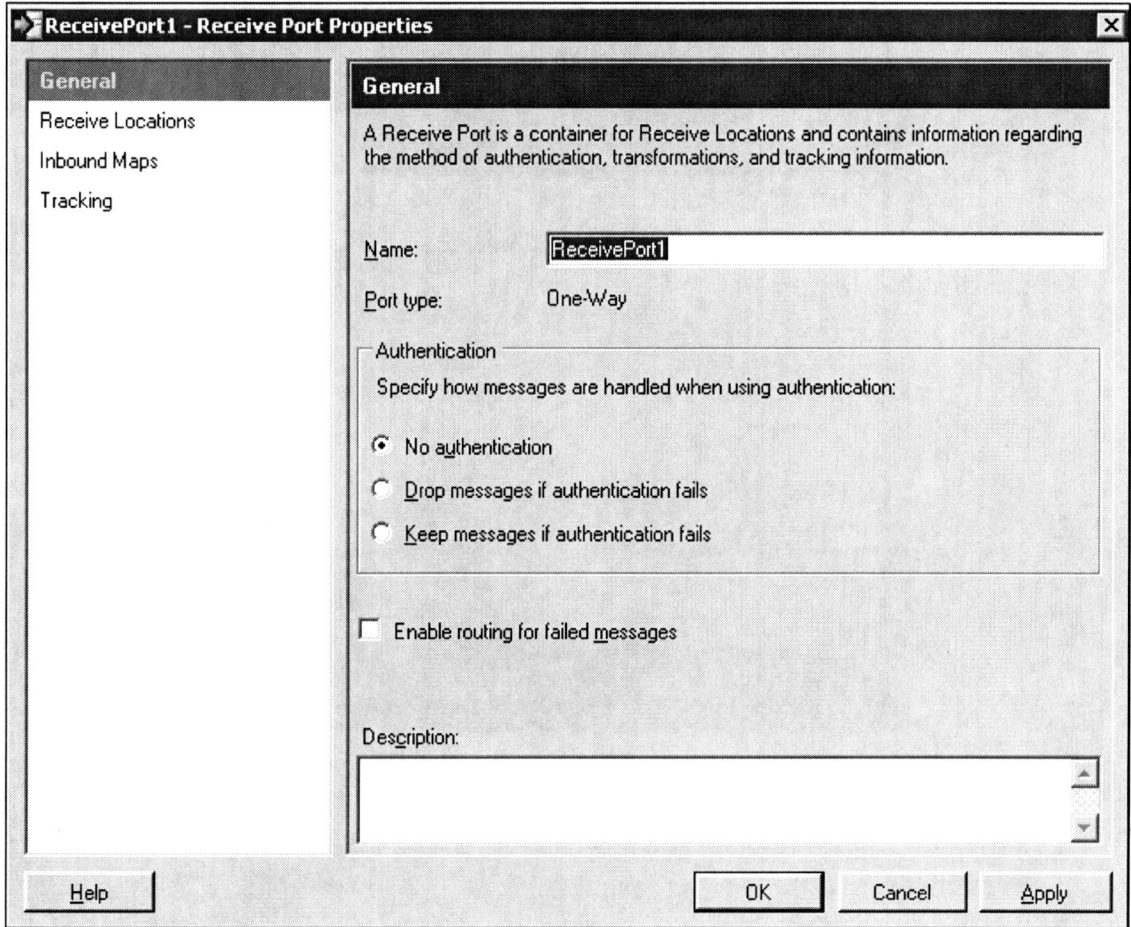

Figure 1-10. Adding a receive port

2. Name the receive port **BTDemoReceivePort** and click the OK button.

3. Add a receive location by right-clicking the Receive Locations folder and selecting the New ➤ One-way Receive Location menu option. Your screen should resemble Figure 1-11.

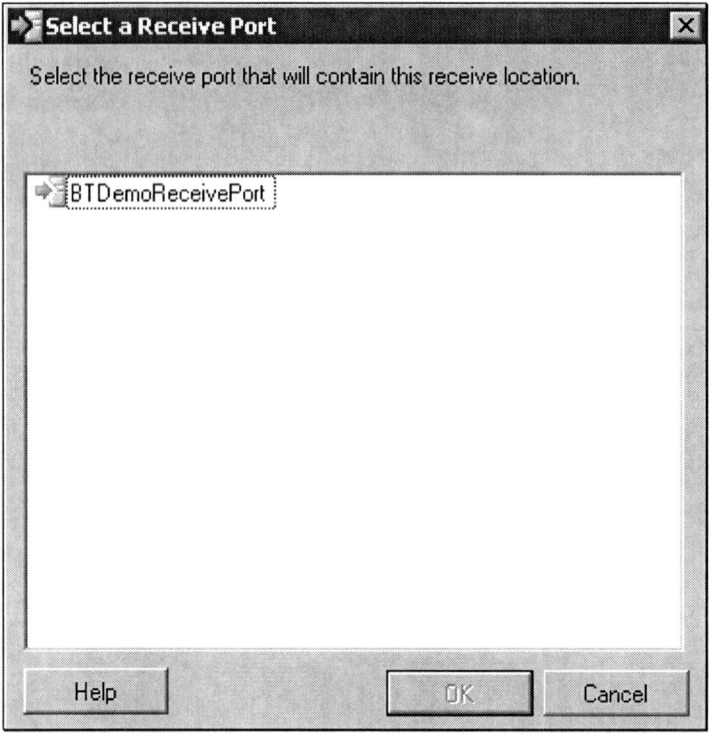

Figure 1-11. Adding a receive location

4. Select BTDemoReceivePort and click the OK button. Your screen should resemble Figure 1-12.

firstPress: Creating, Deploying, and Testing a BizTalk Application   17

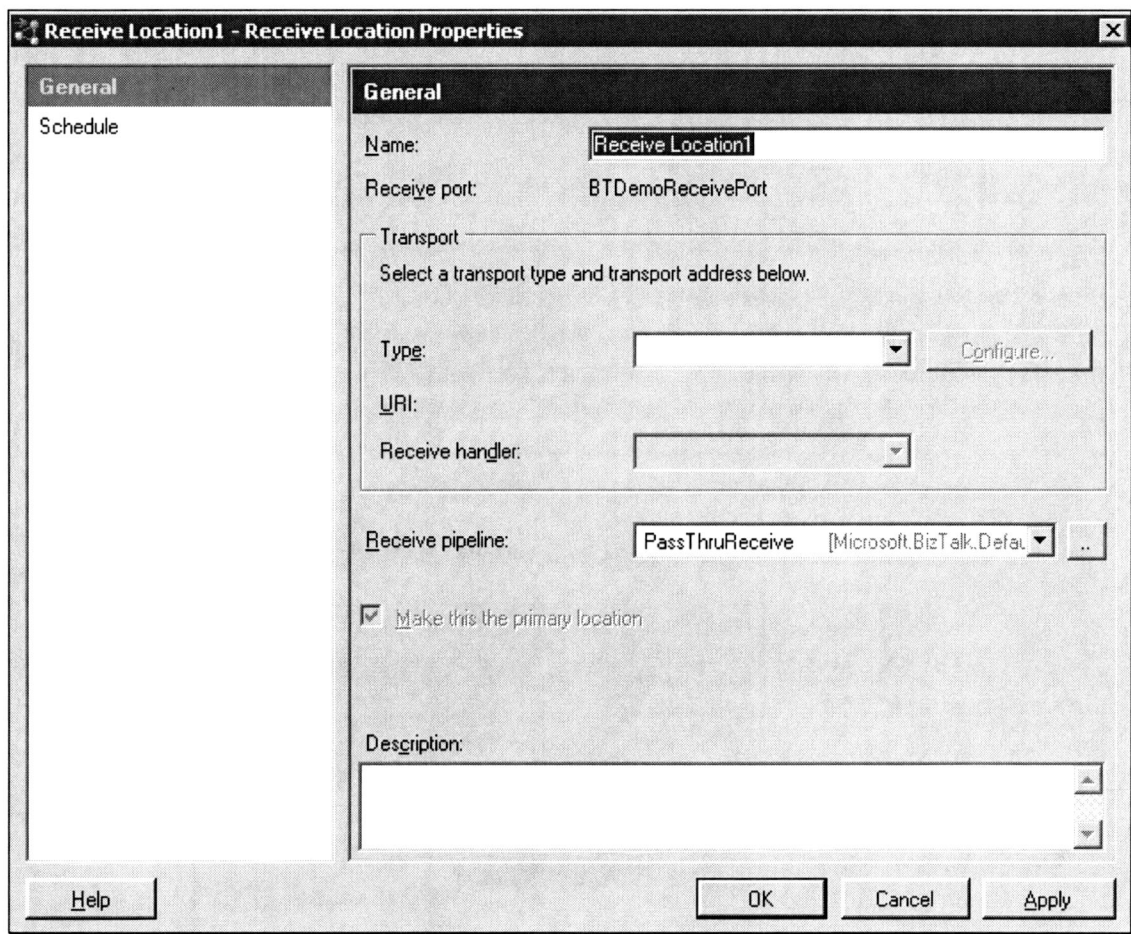

Figure 1-12. Receive location properties

5. Configure the receive location as follows:

Note ➡ In this exercise, you have the option of configuring the receive location to receive a file from an MSMQ queue *or* to receive it from a folder. If you aren't set up to have an XML file placed on the MSMQ queue and to edit/view the contents of the file, use the File Copy example values.

---

18   *firstPress: Creating, Deploying, and Testing a BizTalk Application*

Property	Value (MSMQ Example)	Value (File Copy Example)
Name	BTDemoReceiveLocation	BTDemoReceiveLocation
Transport Type	MSMQ	File
Receive pipeline	XMLReceive	Pass Thru Receive

Note ➡ *Pipelines* enable the transformation of messages during the receipt and sending of messages. The Pass Thru Receive pipeline is used for simple pass-through scenarios when no message processing is necessary; the destination of the message is known; and the message requires no validation, encoding, or disassembling. The XMLReceive pipeline is used to receive and process an XML message.

6a. Configure the Transport by clicking the Configure button.

If you're using the MSMQ example, your screen should look like Figure 1-13.

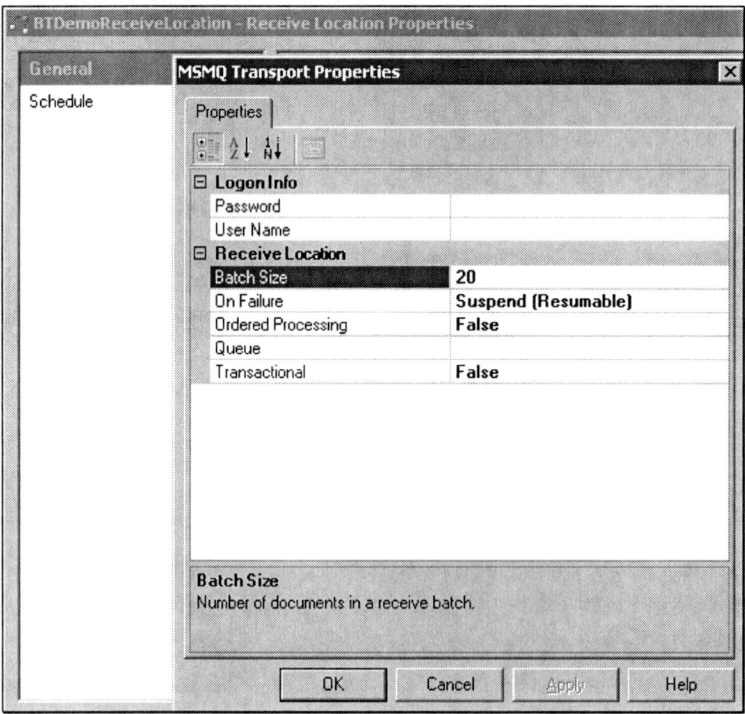

Figure 1-13. MSMQ (receive) Transport Properties

Use the following values to configure the MSMQ Transport Properties, and then click the OK button:

Property	Value
Password	(*Information appropriate for your installation*)
User Name	(*Information appropriate for your installation*)
Queue	(*Information appropriate for your installation*)

6b. If you're using the File Copy example, your screen should resemble Figure 1-14.

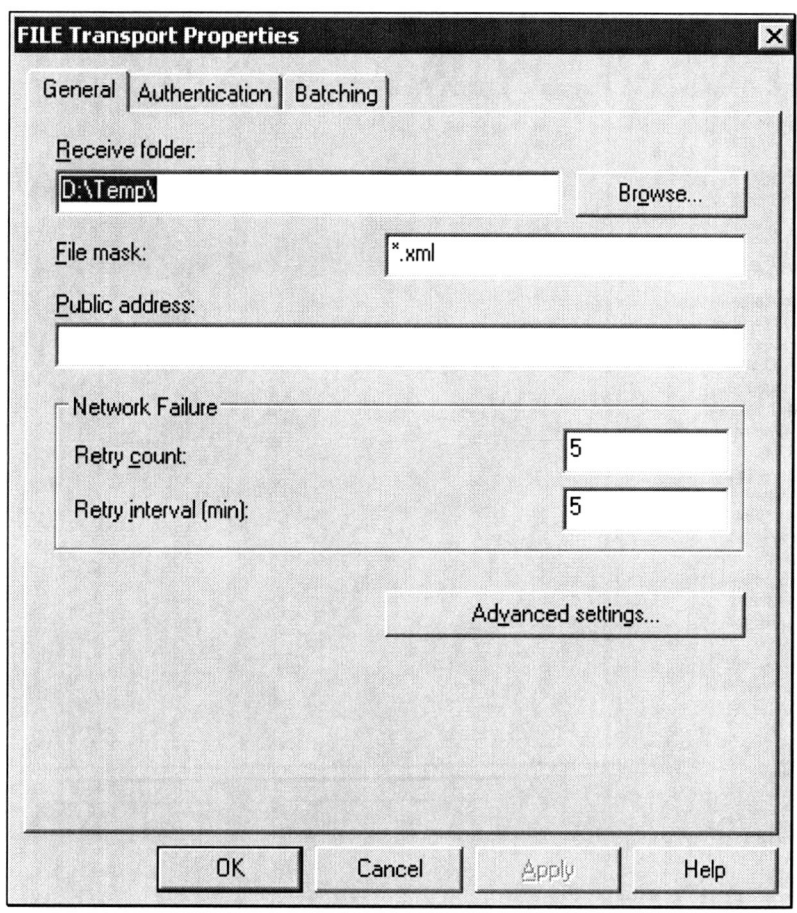

Figure 1-14. File (receive) Transport Properties

20   firstPress: Creating, Deploying, and Testing a BizTalk Application

Use the following information to configure the File Transport Properties, and then click the OK button:

Property	Value
Receive folder	*(Information appropriate for your installation)*

Note ➡ The File mask (in this case, *.xml) is used to determine which files should be processed by the application. Files ending in an extension other than .xml will not be processed, even if they appear in the correct location.

7. Click OK to close the Receive Location Properties dialog box. Your screen should look like Figure 1-15.

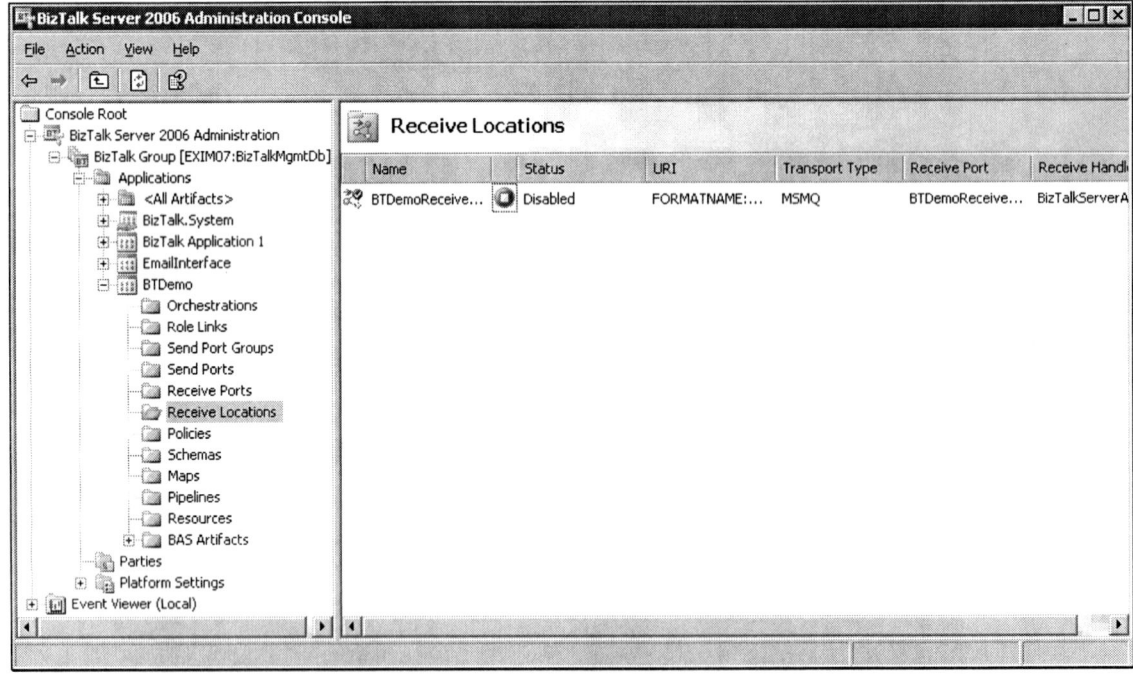

Figure 1-15. BTDemo receive locations

firstPress: Creating, Deploying, and Testing a BizTalk Application 21

8. Enable the receive location by right-clicking the BTDemoReceiveLocation row and selecting the Enable menu option.

Add and Configure a Send Port

Follow these steps to add and configure a send port:

1. Add a send port by right-clicking the Send Ports folder and selecting New ➤ Static One-way Send Port. Your screen should look like Figure 1-16.

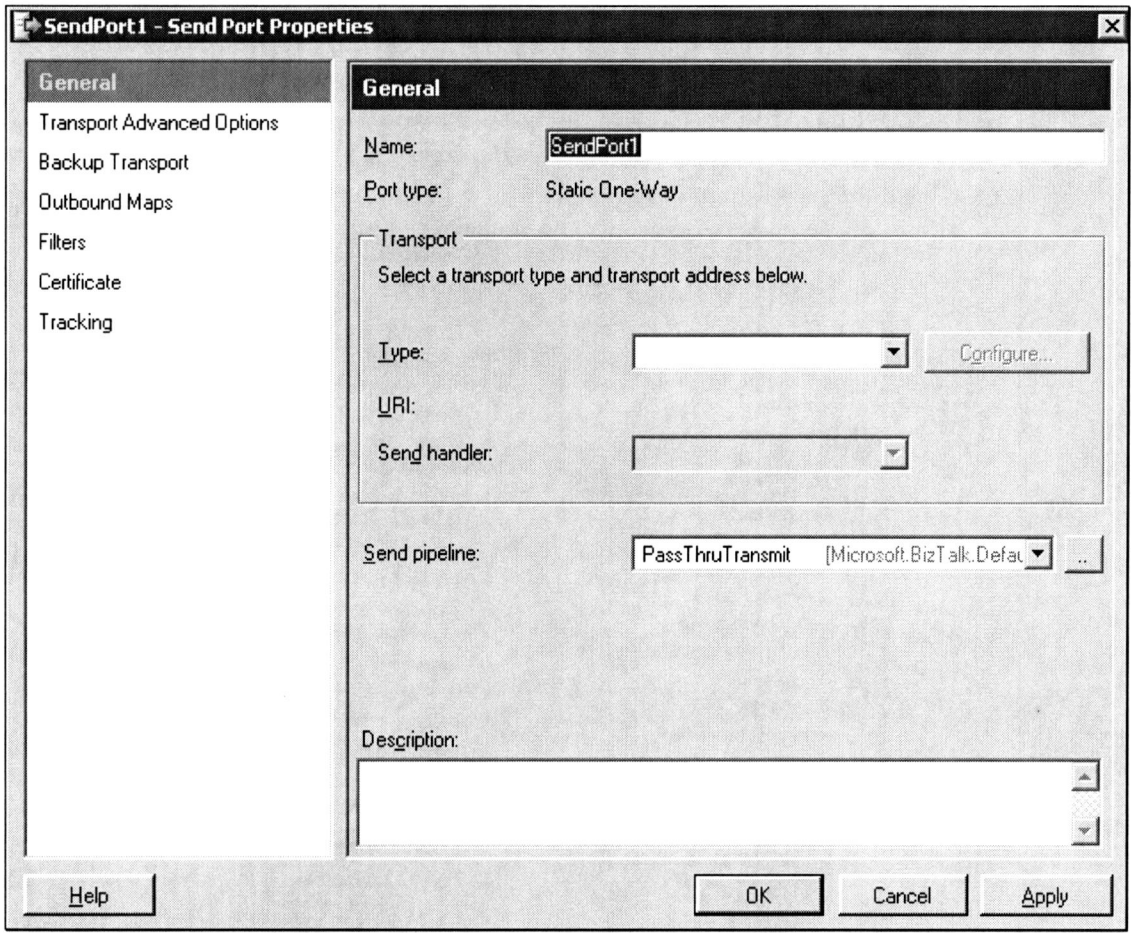

Figure 1-16. Adding a send port

2. Configure the send port as follows:

Property	Value (MSMQ Example)	Value (File Copy Example)
Name	BTDemoSendPort	BTDemoSendPort
Transport Type	MSMQ	File
Send pipeline	XMLTransmit	Pass Thru Transmit

Note ➡ The Pass Thru Transmit pipeline is used when no document processing is required before sending. The XMLTransmit pipeline is used to send an XML message that requires assembly (i.e., converting the message to the proper XML structure based on the properties set in the schema).

3a. Click the Transport Configure button. If you're following the MSMQ example, you should see the screen shown in Figure 1-17.

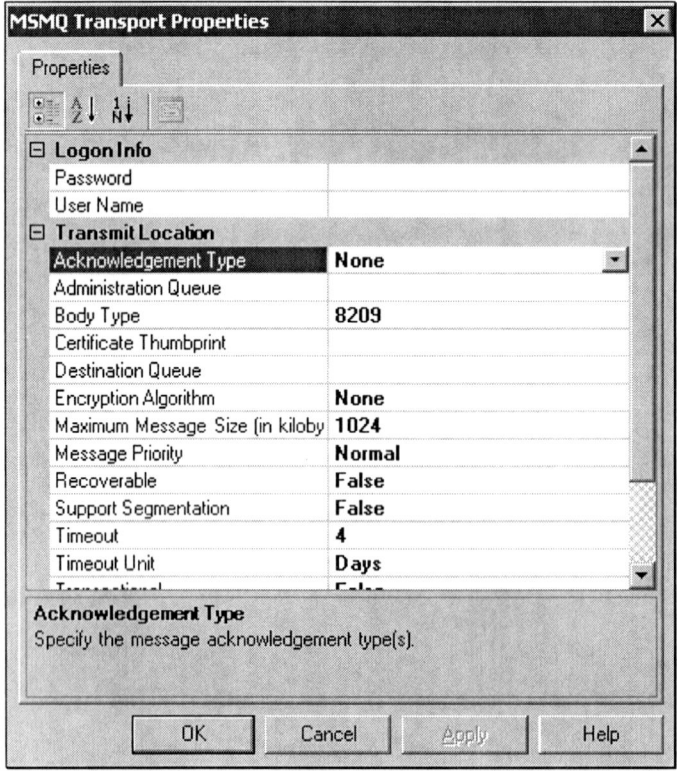

Figure 1-17. MSMQ (send) Transport Properties

firstPress: Creating, Deploying, and Testing a BizTalk Application   23

Configure the MSMQ Transport Properties as follows and then click the OK button:

Property	Value
Password	(*Information appropriate for your installation*)
User Name	(*Information appropriate for your installation*)
Destination Queue	(*Information appropriate for your installation*)

3b. If you're following the File Copy example, your screen will resemble Figure 1-18.

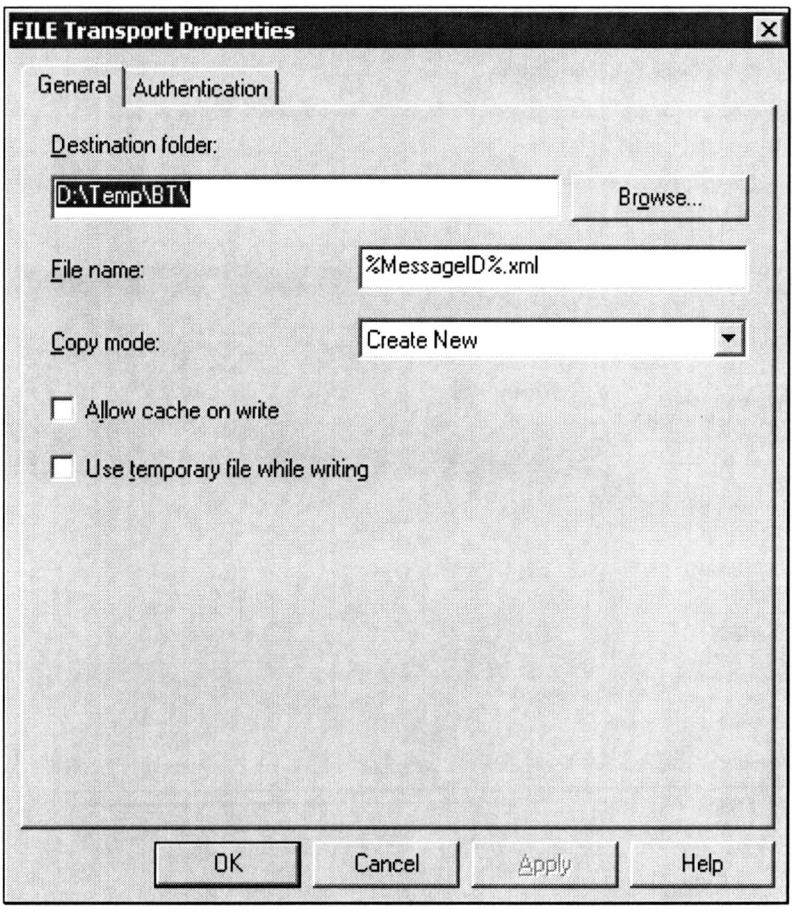

Figure 1-18. File (send) Transport Properties

Loftin

24   *firstPress: Creating, Deploying, and Testing a BizTalk Application*

Configure the File Transport Properties as follows and then click the OK button:

Property	Value
Destination folder	(*Information appropriate for your installation*)

Files copied to the new location will be named as per the File name property.

Note ➡ File Transport allows information processed through a send port to be stored in files. The folder in which the files will be stored is specified by the Destination folder property, and the file name will follow the convention specified by the File name property. The file name mask, %MessageID%, is a way of ensuring that that all files created have a unique name.

4. Click the OK button to close the Send Port Properties dialog. Your screen look like Figure 1-19.

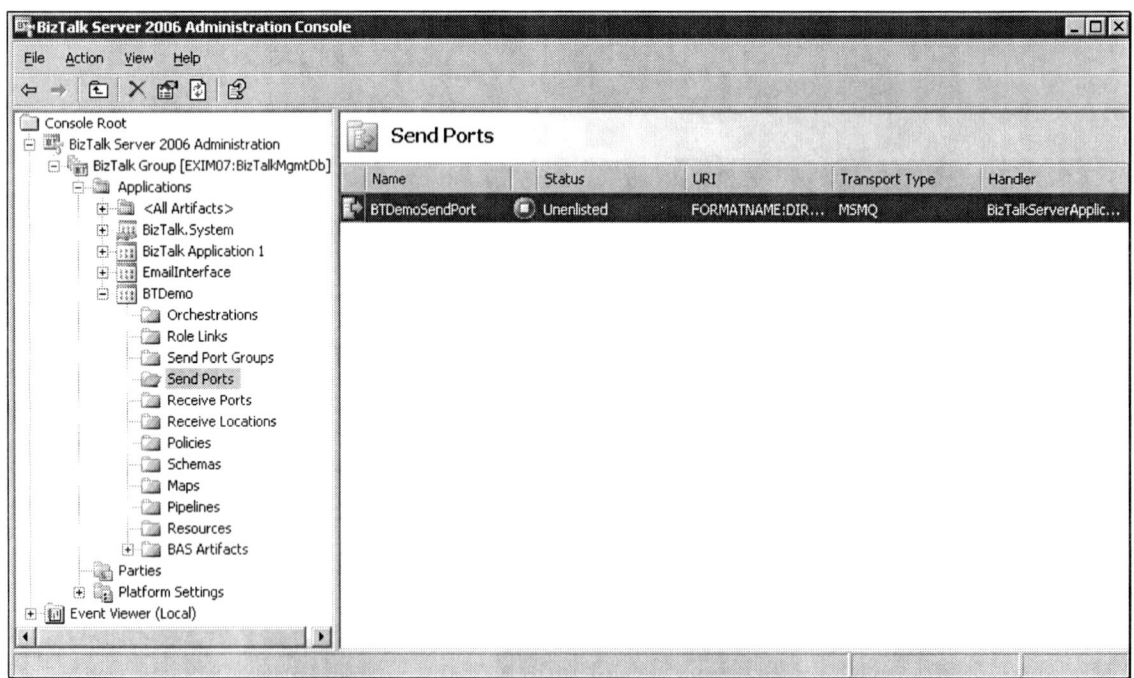

Figure 1-19. BTDemo send ports

5. Start the send port by right-clicking the BTDemoSendPort row and selecting the Start menu option.

Configure the Application

Follow these steps to configure the application:

1. Right-click the BTDemo application node and select the Configure menu option. Your screen should resemble Figure 1-20.

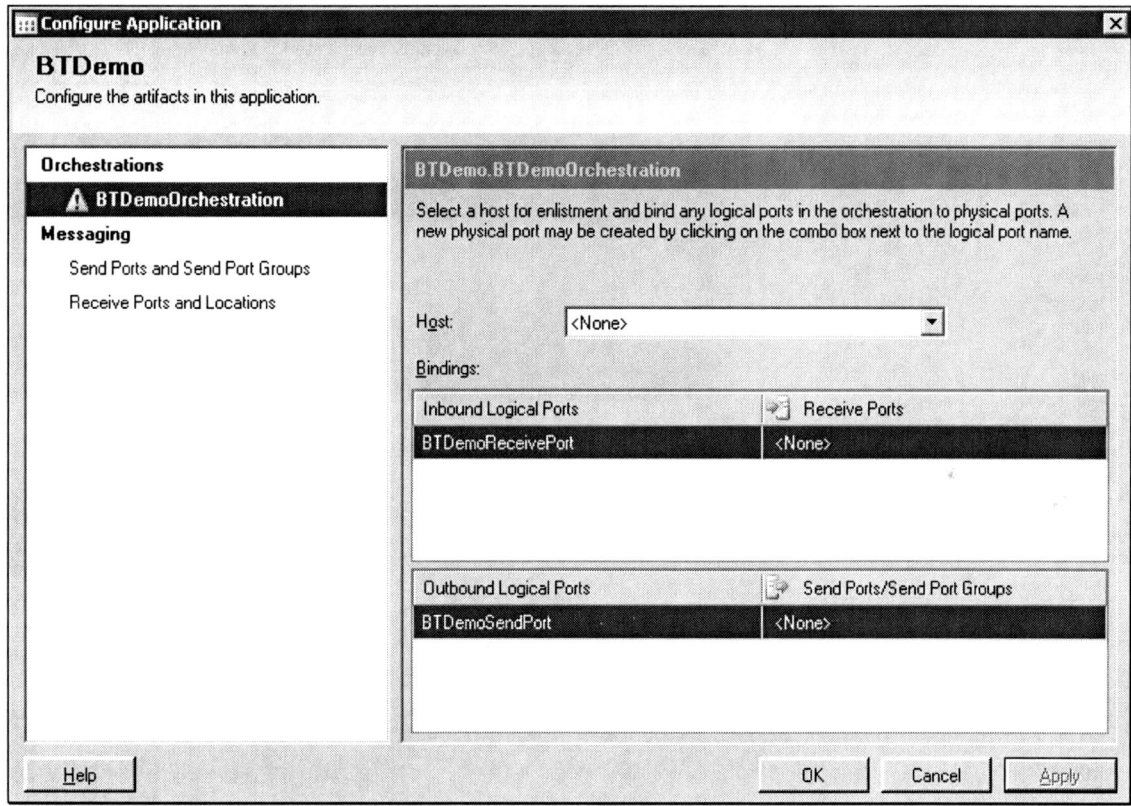

Figure 1-20. Configuring the application

2. Select a host for your application from the drop-down box (BizTalkServerApplication in this example).

3. Assign values to the Inbound Logical Ports and Outbound Logical Ports by selecting from the respective drop-down boxes, as shown in Figure 1-21.

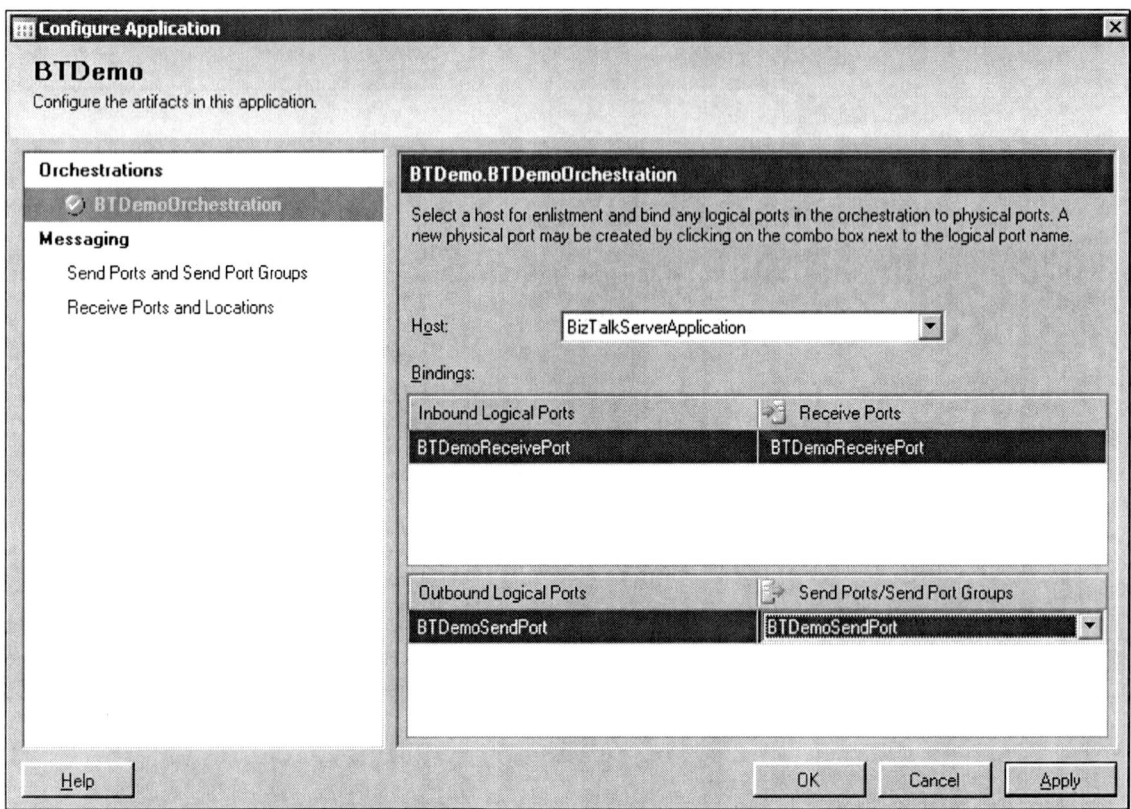

Figure 1-21. Assigning Inbound Logical Ports and Outbound Logical Ports values

---

Note ➡ Ports created in the application during the design process are sometimes referred to as *orchestration ports* or *logical ports*. Ports created in the BizTalk Server Administration console are sometimes referred to as *physical ports*. In any event, the logical ports of the orchestration must be associated with the physical ports of the server.

---

4. Click the OK button to close the Configure Application dialog box.

Launch and Test the Application

Now it's time to launch and test the application:

1. Start the BTDemo application by right-clicking the BTDemo node and selecting the Start menu option.

2. Test the application. If you're using the MSMQ example, you must cause a structurally valid XML message to be placed on the queue specified by the receive location. If you're using the File Copy example, you must cause a valid XML file (with the proper .xml file name extension) to be placed in the folder specified by the receive location.

   Once you are comfortable that the application is functioning properly, you can make adjustments in the receive location and send port to receive an XML document via MSMQ and have it written to a file directory *or* receive an XML document in a folder and have it written to an MSMQ queue, and so forth.

3. Bring the BTDemo application to a full stop.

4. Close the BizTalk Administration console.

Summary

Congratulations! You have completed your first BizTalk project. Even though the project was simple, it introduced you to some very important tools (Visual Studio 2005 and the BizTalk Server Administration console) and artifacts (orchestrations, messages, and ports). In subsequent phases, you will be introduced to new tools and artifacts, and you will build upon the knowledge that you have gained in this phase.

Before moving on to the next phase, let's review what you learned in this phase:

- Visual Studio is used to create a BizTalk Server project by using the BizTalk Server Project template.

- BizTalk Server projects are composed of several different file types: orchestrations, map files, pipeline files, and schema files. This phase introduced you to orchestrations.

- An orchestration is a BizTalk program. It is the means by which you include processing logic in your BizTalk project. However, instead of using individual programming statements, you program with graphical objects. Consequently, a BizTalk program is a diagram of interconnected graphical objects.

- Systems communicate with each other by exchanging messages. There are various types of messages—most notably, XML or flat file.

- Messages arrive in the BizTalk Server address space or are sent from the BizTalk Server address space via ports. Ports can be receive-only, send-only, or bidirectional.

- Ports are assigned a port type depending on the message type.

- Once defined, ports are added to the orchestration by placing a Port shape graphical object on the orchestration diagram.

- BizTalk projects are compiled into .NET assemblies. These assemblies must have a strong name.

- The BizTalk Server Administration console is used to install, configure, launch, and troubleshoot a BizTalk Server project.

- Ports that have not been configured in the BizTalk Server project must be configured in the Administration console. Using the Administration Console to configure ports allows you to change port settings without recompiling and redeploying your BizTalk Server project.

PHASE 2

Working with Schemas

Now that you understand some of the BizTalk tools and how to use them, let's increase the complexity of the demonstration project.

In this phase, you will create a schema that will define the structure of the message you will be processing. You will validate the schema and use it to generate an instance file that conforms to the schema. You will then create an orchestration that uses data embedded within the incoming message to implement a business rule. Finally, you will deploy the application to the BizTalk server and test it.

The schema you create will be used to define the structure of an XML file that is used to generate an e-mail message such as the following:

```xml
<?xml version="1.0" encoding="UTF-8"?>
<emailservice>
        <transx command="send" />
        <send>
                <fromaddr>FromAddr</fromaddr>
                <toaddr>ToAddr</toaddr>
                <cc>Cc</cc>
                <bcc>Bcc</bcc>
                <subject>Subject</subject>
                <body>Body</body>
                <bodyformat>text</bodyformat>
                <attachments>
                        <attachment filename="file1.pdf" />
                        <attachment filename="file2.pdf" />
                </attachments>
        </send>
</emailservice>
```

Again, the tasks that must be performed in Visual Studio 2005 and BizTalk Server Administration console appear in their own sections to assist you in knowing when to transfer from one tool to the other.

Note ➡ This phase takes approximately one hour to complete.

Visual Studio 2005 Tasks

The tasks that you will perform using Visual Studio 2005 are covered in detail in the sections that follow.

Add a Schema to the Project

Follow these steps to add a schema to the project:

1. Launch Visual Studio 2005 and open the BTDemo project.
2. Add a new item to the project by right-clicking the BTDemo project in Solution Explorer and selecting Add ➤ New Item. Your screen should resemble Figure 2-1.

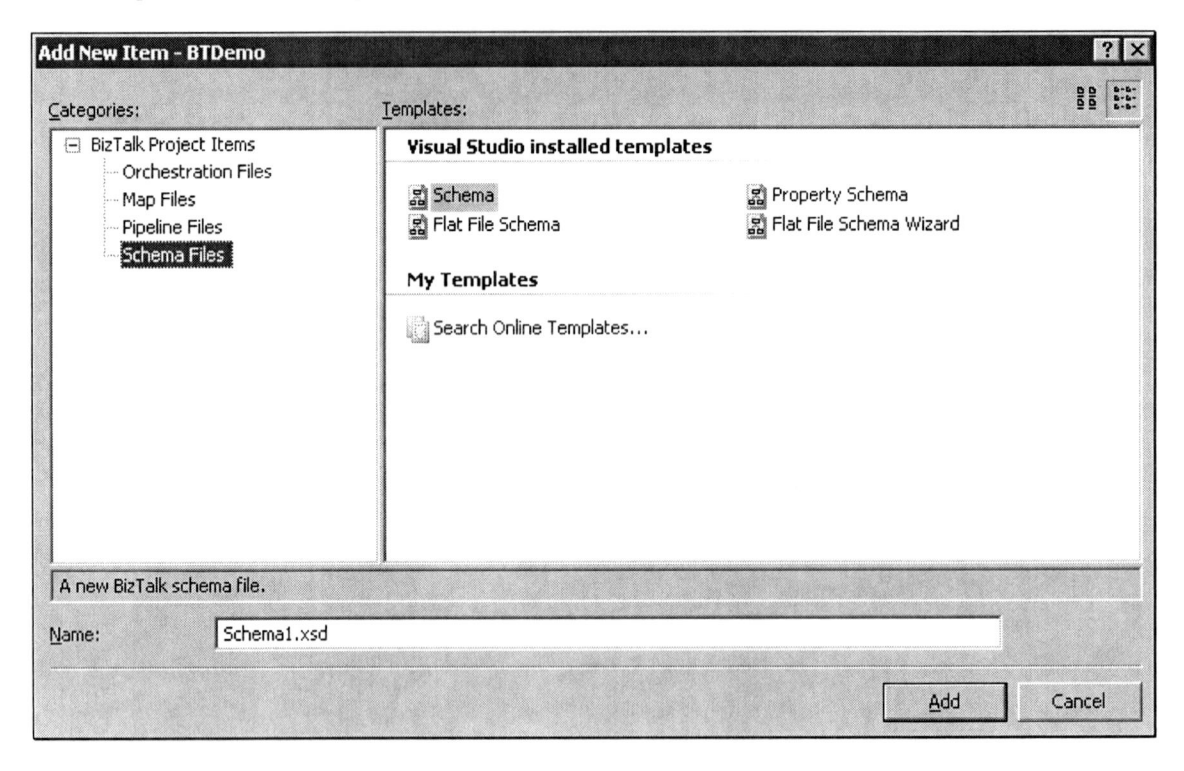

Figure 2-1. Adding a new schema

firstPress: Working with Schemas	*31*

3. In the left pane select Schema Files, and in the right pane select Schema. Name the schema file **BTDemoEmailSchema.xsd**. Click the Add button to add the schema to the project. You should see a screen like that shown in Figure 2-2.

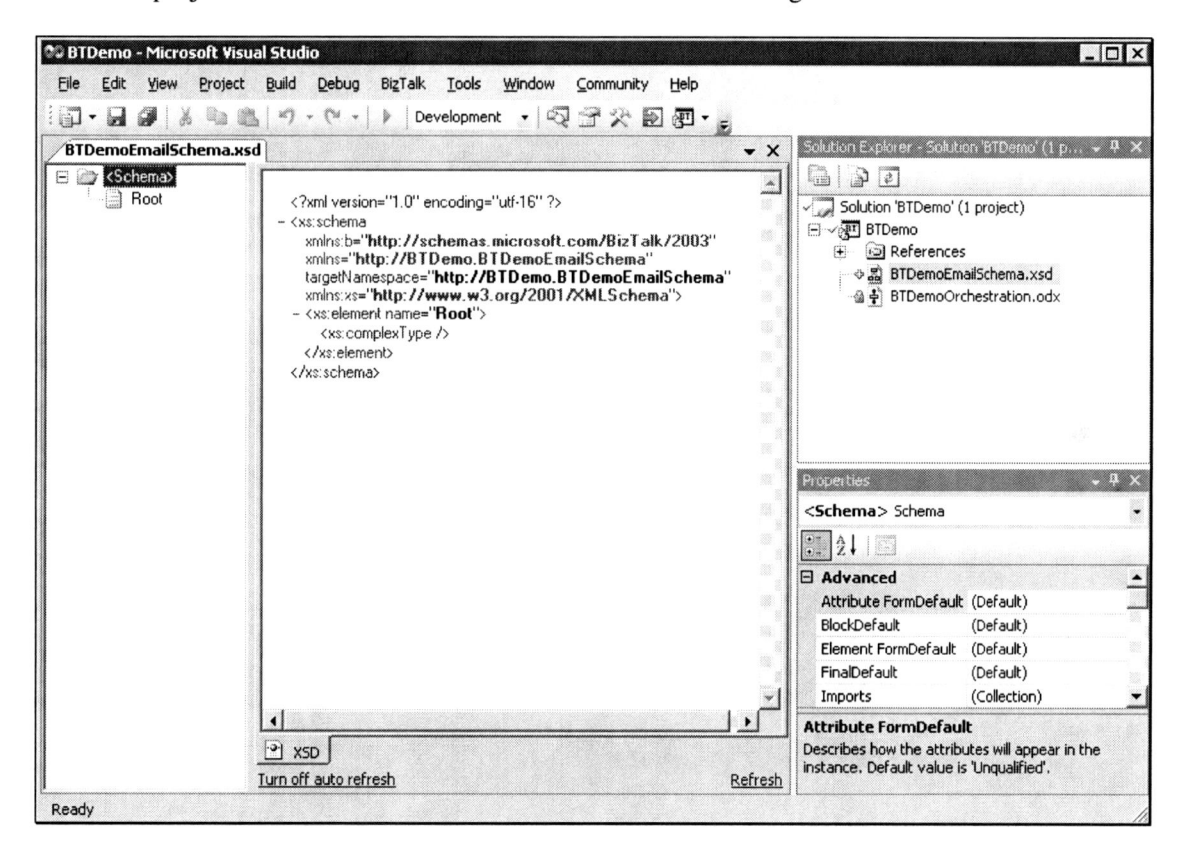

Figure 2-2. Initial schema definition

4. Right-click the Root node and rename it **emailservice**.

5. Create a child node under the emailservice node by right-clicking the emailservice node and selecting Insert Schema Node ➤ Child Record. Rename the node you just created as **transx**.

6. Create a second child record node under the emailservice node and rename the newly created node **send**. Your screen should resemble Figure 2-3.

Loftin

firstPress: Working with Schemas

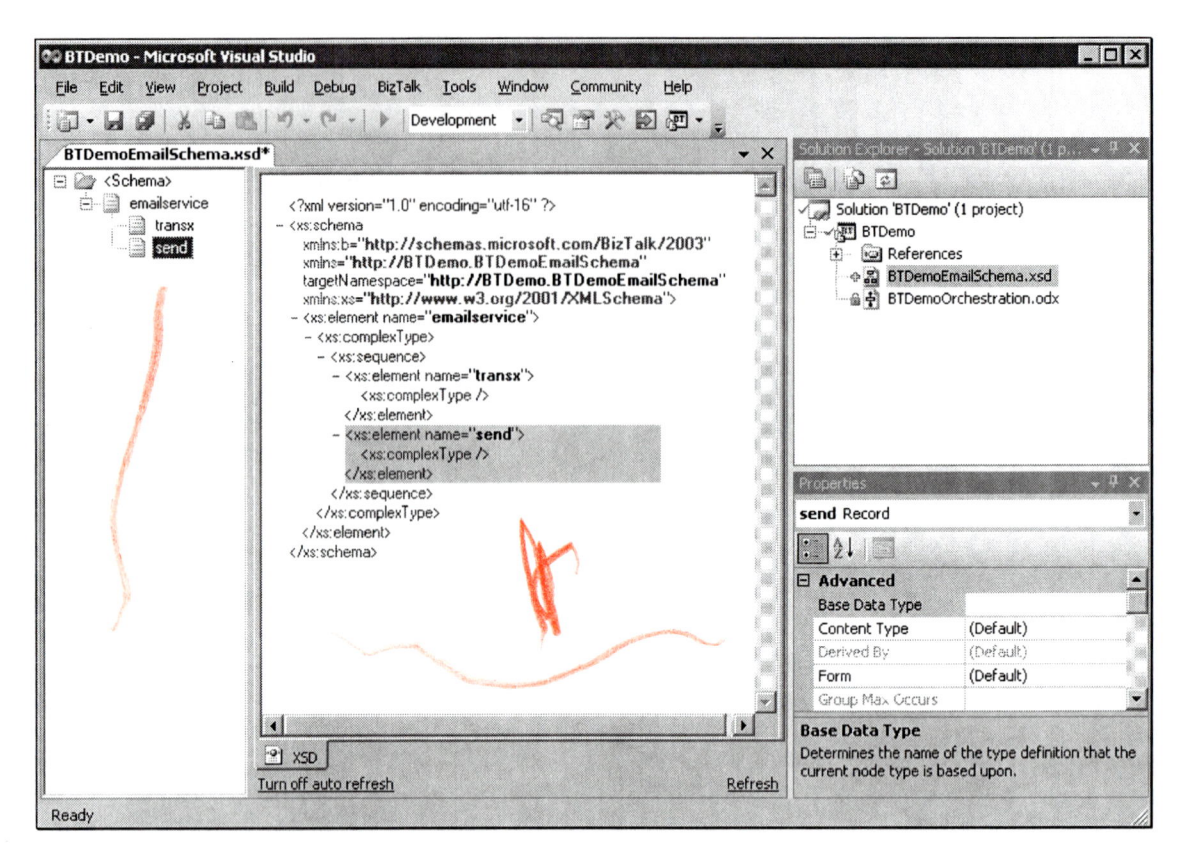

Figure 2-3. Adding a child node to the schema

7. Add a field attribute to the transx node by right-clicking the transx node and selecting Insert Schema Node ➤ Child Field Attribute. Name the newly created node **command**.

8. Using the process previously described, add the following child record nodes to the send node: fromaddr, toaddr, cc, bcc, subject, body, bodyformat, and attachments. Your screen should resemble Figure 2-4.

firstPress: Working with Schemas 33

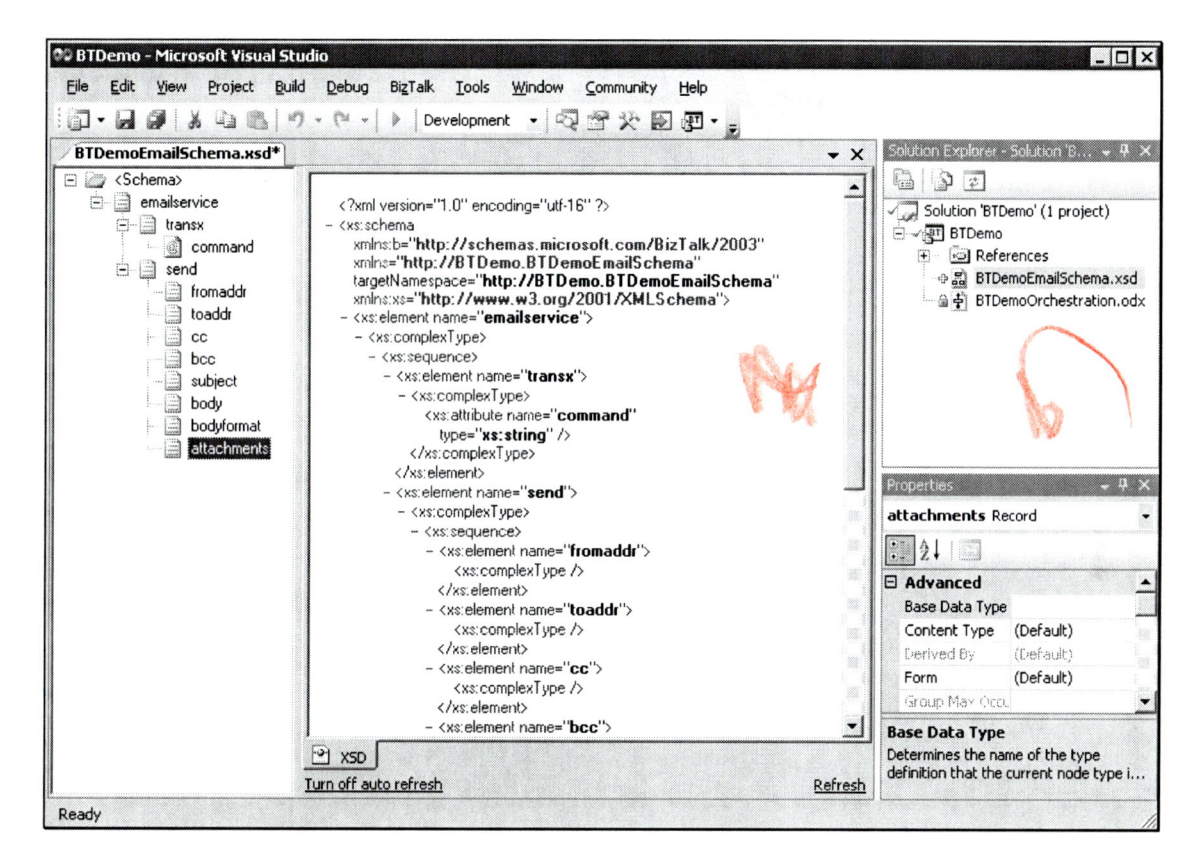

Figure 2-4. Schema definition with child nodes

9. Add a child record node to the attachments node named **attachment**.

10. Add a child field attribute to the attachment node named **filename**. Your screen should now look like Figure 2-5.

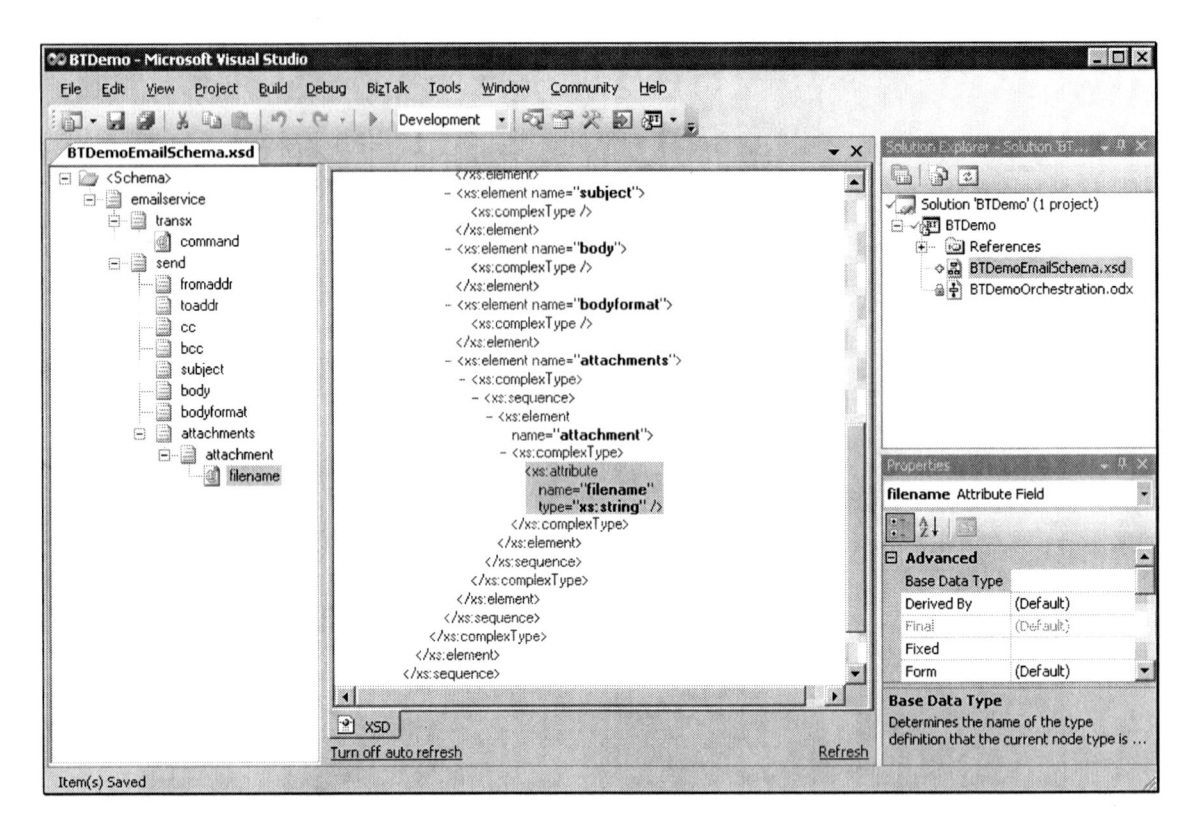

Figure 2-5. Adding a child field attribute node

11. Validate the schema by right-clicking the BTDemoEmailSchema.xsd node in Solution Explorer and selecting the Validate Schema menu option. Results of the validation will be displayed in the Output window. If the validation was not successful, review your work and revise until the schema validates successfully.

The schema defines the structure of the document being processed. It can be used

- To generate an instance of an XML document that conforms to the schema. This instance document can be given to developers to let them know the format of the XML documents their applications should be creating in order to be processed correctly by BizTalk.
- To validate that documents coming into BizTalk are properly formatted.
- In an orchestration, to make decisions based on the content of documents described by the schema.

Generate an Instance Document

To generate an instance document, follow these steps:

1. Right-click the BTDemoEmailSchema.xsd node in Solution Explorer and select the Properties menu option. Your screen should resemble Figure 2-6.

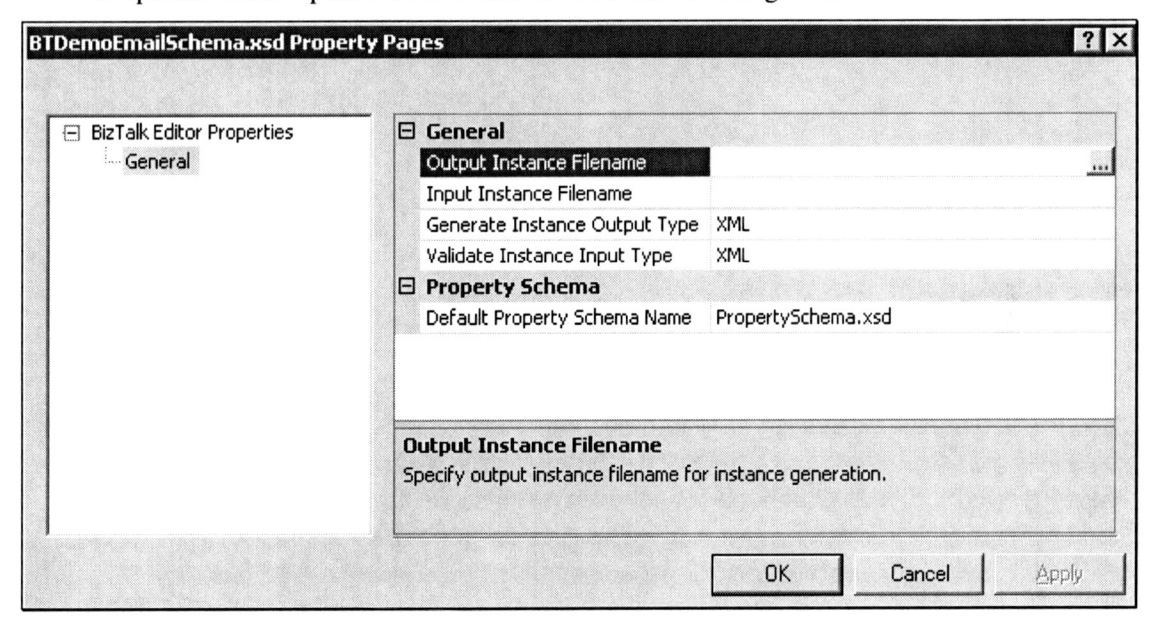

Figure 2-6. Generating a schema instance document

2. Specify the file name of the instance document to be generated by entering it in the Output Instance Filename text box. For the purposes of this example, set the file name to be BTDemoMailMsg.xml. Click the OK button.

3. Right-click the BTDemoEmailSchema.xsd node in Solution Explorer and select the Generate Instance menu option. You can use Internet Explorer or Notepad to view the contents of the generated file, which should resemble the following:

```xml
<ns0:emailservice xmlns:ns0="http://BTDemo.BTDemoEmailSchema">
 <transx command="command_0" />
 <send>
  <fromaddr />
  <toaddr />
  <cc />
  <bcc />
  <subject />
  <body />
  <bodyformat />
  <attachments>
    <attachment filename="filename_0" />
  </attachments>
 </send>
</ns0:emailservice>
```

Note ➡ The generated instance has, as its root node, <ns0:emailservice>. To remove the ns0 prefix, you will need to set the Target Namespace property of the Schema node to blank; however, be aware that doing so has consequences. It could affect processing within BizTalk, because BizTalk uses the namespace and the root node to uniquely identify messages. And, because processing within BizTalk is dependent on a unique message identity, some messages could be processed incorrectly if uniqueness isn't preserved.

Validate the Instance Document

You can use the schema you just created to validate that an XML document conforms to the schema, by following these steps:

1. Display the Property Pages dialog box for the schema by right-clicking the BTDemoEmailSchema.xsd node in Solution Explorer and selecting the Properties menu option (see Figure 2-7).

firstPress: Working with Schemas

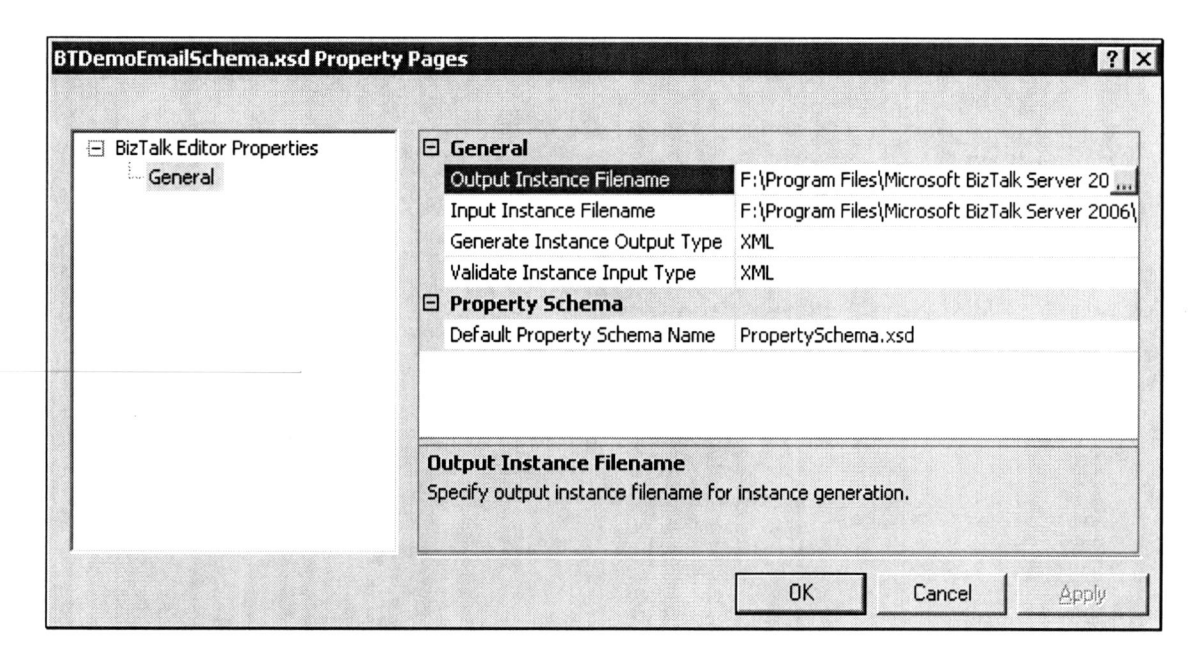

Figure 2-7. Setting the input instance file name

2. Enter the name of the file to be validated in the Input Instance Filename text box. For the purposes of this exercise, set the Input Instance Filename to be the same as the Output Instance Filename. Click the OK button.

3. Validate the instance document by right-clicking the BTDemoEmailSchema.xsd node in Solution Explorer and selecting the Validate Instance menu option. Your screen should look like Figure 2-8.

38 firstPress: Working with Schemas

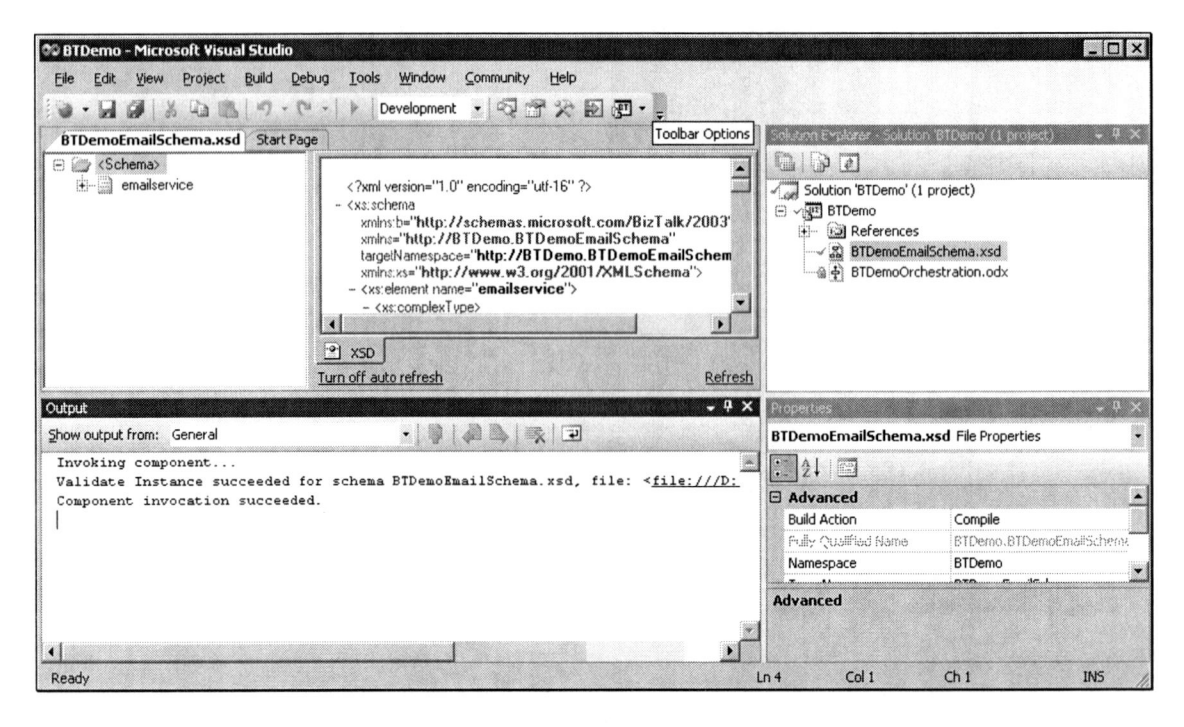

Figure 2-8. Schema validation results

The results of the validation will display in the Output window. In some cases, the validation may fail on a generated instance. However, in the case of this example, the validation should succeed.

Force a Validation Failure

To demonstrate a validation failure, you will create a required attribute in the schema and repeat the validation.

1. Expand the emailservice ➤ transx schema node.

2. Add a new attribute to the schema by right-clicking the transx node and selecting Insert Schema Node ➤ Child Field Attribute. Name the new attribute **datetime**.

3. Set the Use Requirement property of the datetime attribute to be Required. Your screen should resemble Figure 2-9.

Loftin

firstPress: Working with Schemas 39

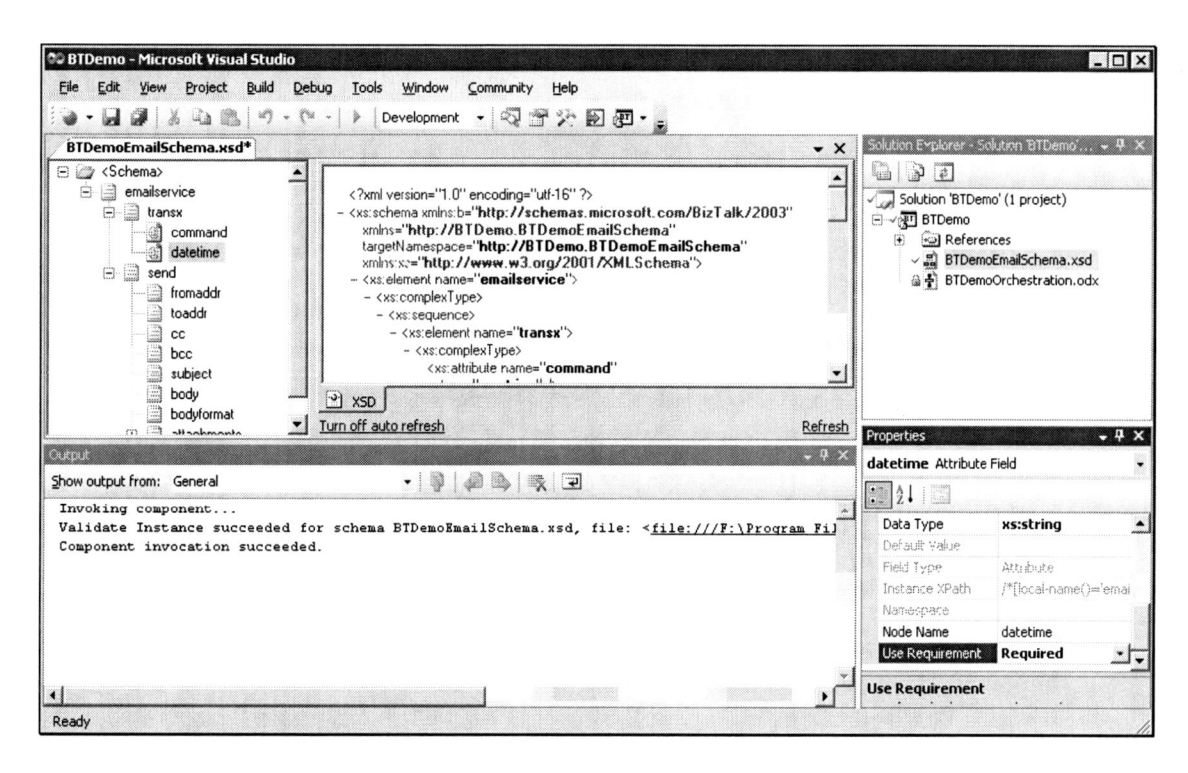

Figure 2-9. Setting the Use Requirement property to Required

4. Validate the instance as previously described. This time you should get a failure because there is no datetime attribute in the input instance document, and you have indicated that datetime is a required attribute. The contents of the Output window should be as follows:

Invoking component...
F:\Program Files\Microsoft BizTalk Server 2006\Projects\BTDemo\BTDemoMailMsg.xml: error BEC2004: **The required attribute 'datetime' is missing.**
F:\Program Files\Microsoft BizTalk Server 2006\Projects\BTDemo\BTDemo\BTDemoEmailSchema.xsd: error BEC2004: Validate Instance failed for schema BTDemoEmailSchema.xsd, file: <file:///F:\Program Files\Microsoft BizTalk Server 2006\Projects\BTDemo\BTDemoMailMsg.xml>.
Component invocation succeeded.

5. Generate a new instance document and validate it. You will see that the validation error goes away.

Promote a Node

An orchestration will normally make decisions by using data embedded within a message. To do this, the orchestration must know how the message is structured. And, since a schema defines the structure of a message, you will be using a schema as part of your orchestration. To make the data in a message available to an orchestration, the node in the schema that contains the data must be either promoted or distinguished.

Note ➡ Data that has been *distinguished* can only be used within an orchestration, whereas data that has been *promoted* can be used in orchestrations, pipelines, ports, and so forth. However, promoted data is limited to 255 characters, whereas distinguished data has no such character limit.

In this example, you will promote the subject node:

1. Right-click the subject node. Notice that the Promote ➤ Quick Promotion menu option has been disabled. This is because the Content Type property of the subject node is not Simple Content.

2. Change the Content Type property of the subject node to Simple Content.

3. Promote the subject node by right-clicking it and selecting Promote ➤ Quick Promotion. Because this is the first time that you are promoting a node, a prompt will display, informing you that a property schema will be created, as shown in Figure 2-10.

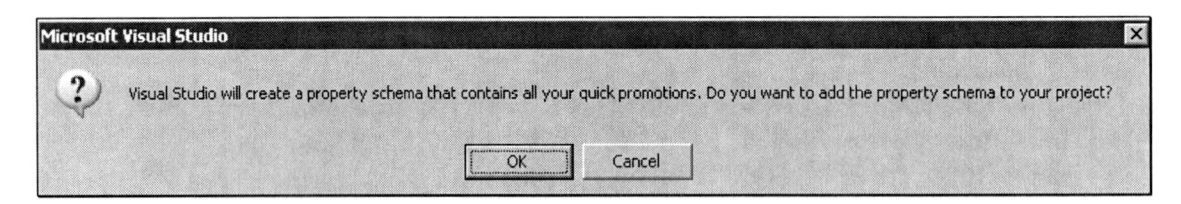

Figure 2-10. Property schema creation prompt

4. Click the OK button. You will notice that the Property Schema file, PropertySchema.xsd, has been added to Solution Explorer.

5. Open the property schema by double-clicking it. Notice that the subject node has been added, as shown in Figure 2-11.

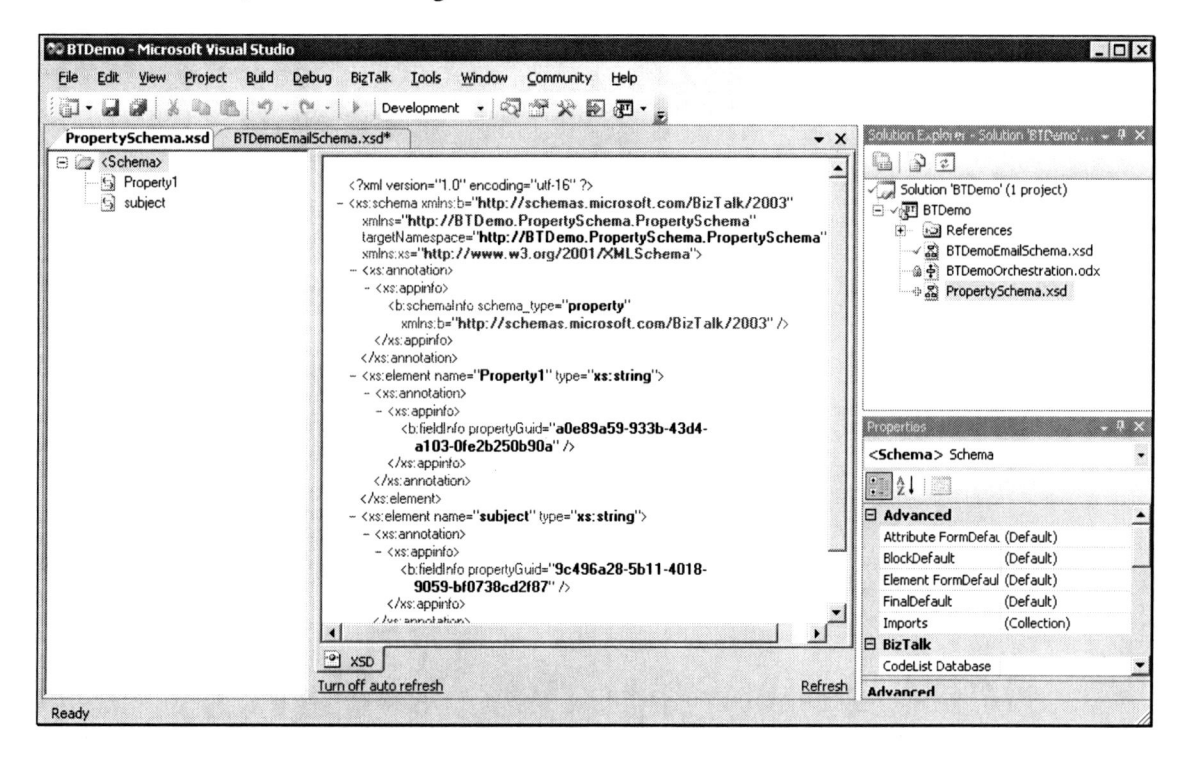

Figure 2-11. The subject node has been added to the property schema.

Also notice that the Property1 node was automatically created. This node can be deleted.

Assign the Schema to a Message

In Phase 1, you created a message. However, that message was not associated with a schema. You will now associate the message to BTDemoSchema.

1. Open the orchestration with the Orchestration View displayed, as shown in Figure 2-12.

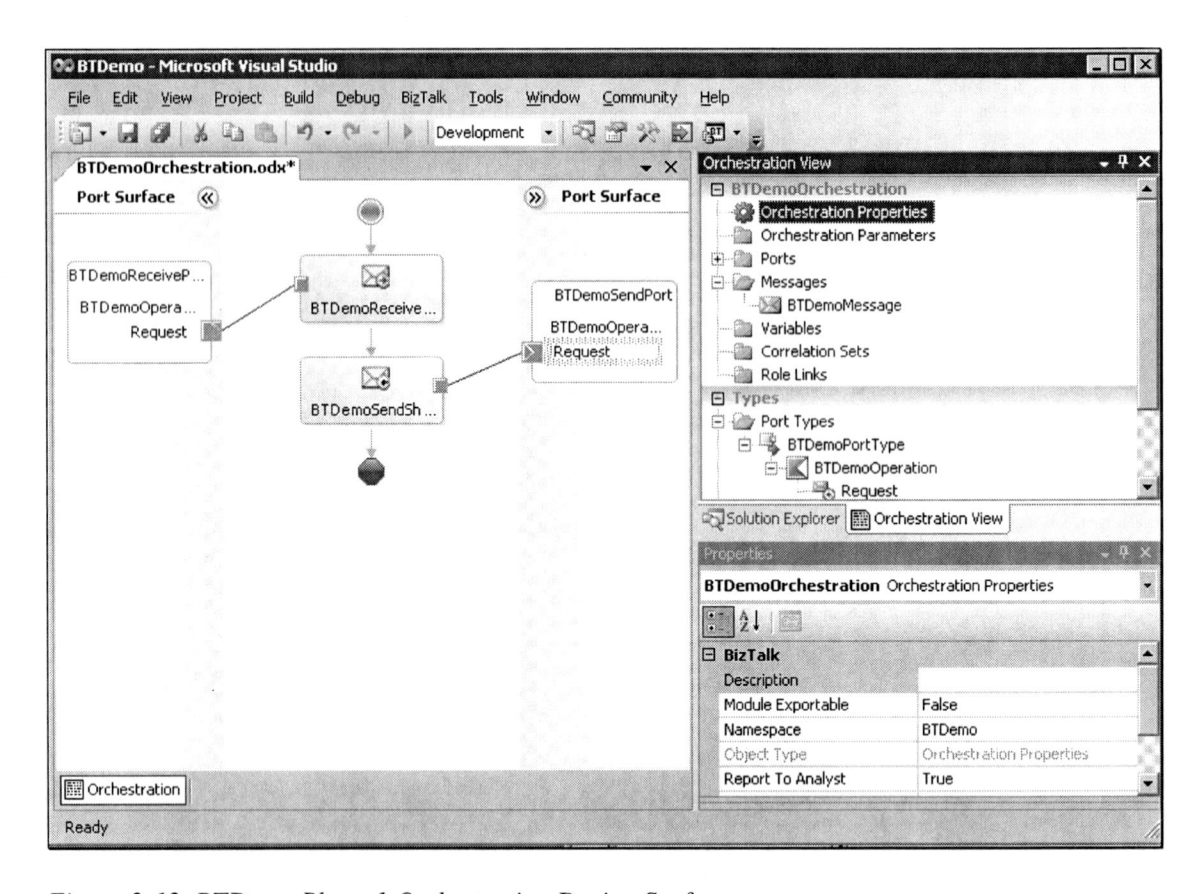

Figure 2-12. BTDemo Phase 1 Orchestration Design Surface

2. Delete the connectors from the Port shapes to the Send and Receive shapes by right-clicking them and selecting Delete. Your screen should now look like Figure 2-13.

firstPress: Working with Schemas 43

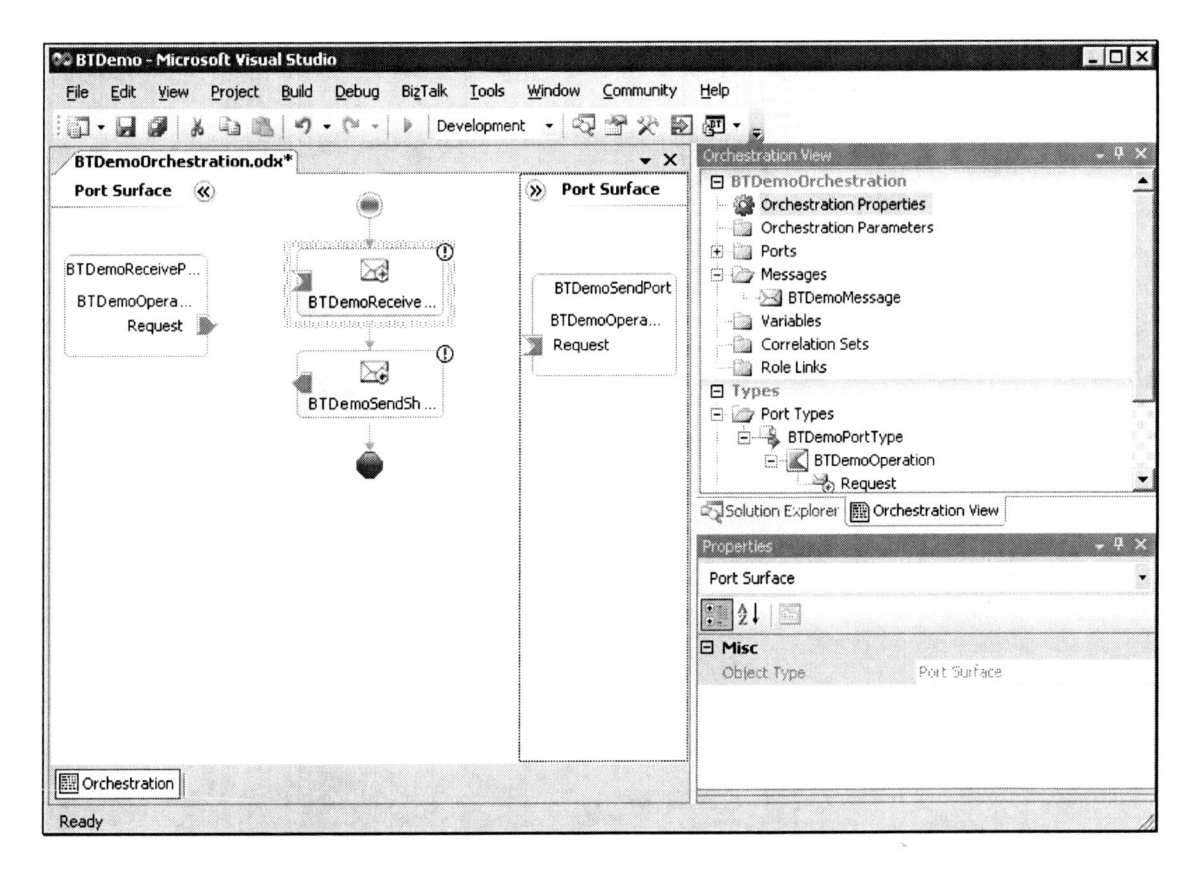

Figure 2-13. After the shape connectors are deleted

Note ➡ The orchestration editor will not permit a Send or Receive shape to bind to a Send or Receive port unless the message type of the port's port type matches the message type of the shape's message. Therefore, the connectors that bind the Send or Receive shape to its respective port must be deleted before either message type can be changed.

3. In the Orchestration View, change the Message Type property for BTDemoMessage to be Schemas ➤ BTDemo.BTDemoEmailSchema.

Loftin

4. Update the Message Type property of BTDemoPortType so that it points to the new schema (Schemas ➤ BTDemo.BTDemoEmailSchema) by selecting Port Types ➤ BTDemoPortType ➤ BTDemoOperation ➤ Request in the Orchestration View window.

5. Reconnect BTDemoReceivePortShape to BTDemoReceiveShape and BTDemoSendPortShape to BTDemoSendShape.

6. Save the project.

Use the Message in the Orchestration

The orchestration will be modified to implement the following business rule:

> *If the subject node of the incoming message is blank, terminate the orchestration and generate an error message. If the subject is not blank, write the file to a send port.*

To implement this rule, you must add a Decide shape and a Terminate shape to the orchestration. These tasks are outlined in the sections that follow.

Add and Configure a Decide Shape

Add a Decide shape to the orchestration between BTDemoReceiveShape and BTDemoSendShape. Your screen should now look like Figure 2-14.

firstPress: Working with Schemas 45

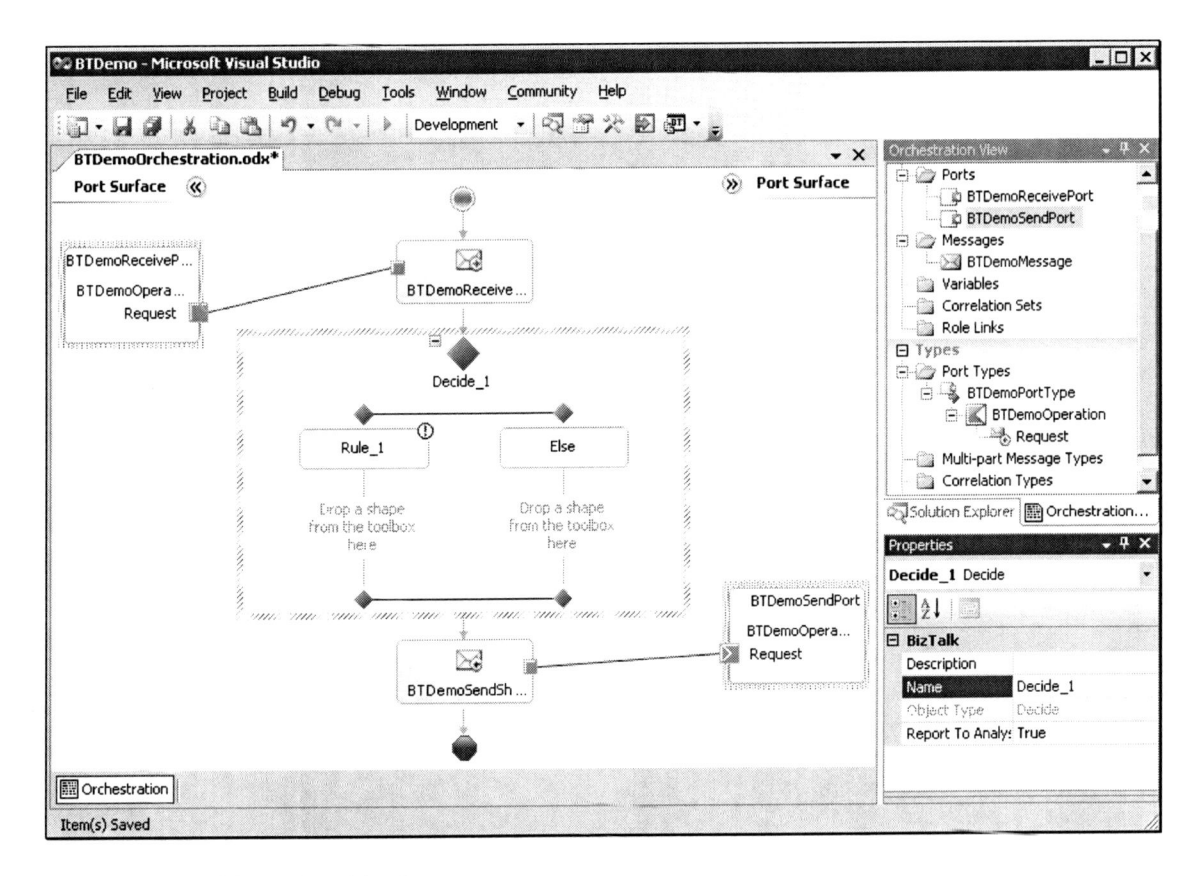

Figure 2-14. Adding a Decide shape

You will use the Decide shape to implement the following business rule:

If the subject field of the message is blank, throw an exception.

Follow these steps to implement the business rule:

1. Rename Decide_1 and Rule_1 as **BTDemoDecideShape** and **BTDemo: Subject Not Blank**, respectively.

2. Open the BizTalk Expression Editor by right-clicking the rule and selecting the Edit Boolean Expression menu option (see Figure 2-15).

Loftin

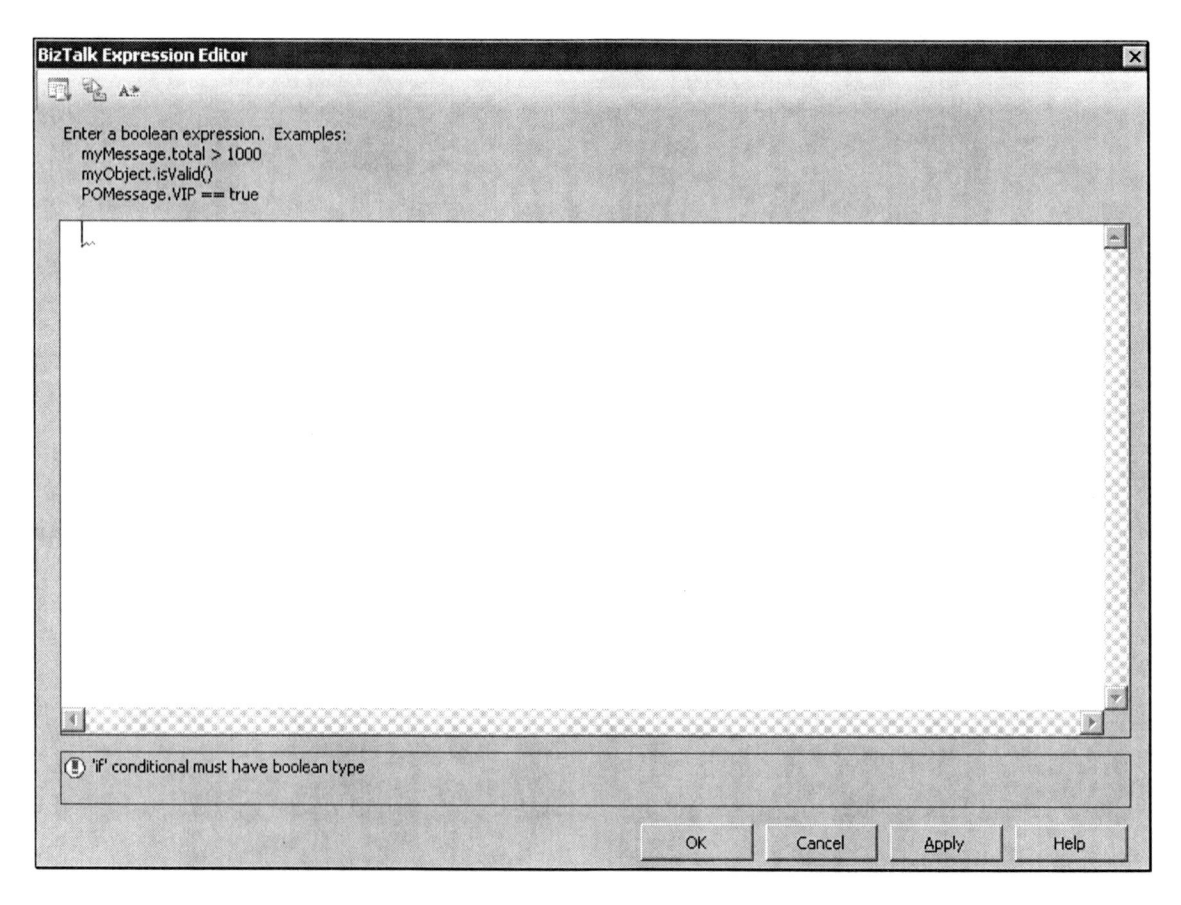

Figure 2-15. The BizTalk Expression Editor

3. Type the name of the message: **BTDemoMessage** (. IntelliSense will present a drop-down list of valid options. Because you have promoted the subject node of the schema, one of the options is BTDemo.PropertySchema.subject. Select that option. If the BTDemo.PropertySchema.subject option does not appear, it is because you haven't saved your work.

4. Enter the following full expression:

BTDemoMessage(BTDemo.PropertySchema.subject) != ""

5. Click OK to close the BizTalk Expression Editor.

firstPress: Working with Schemas					47

Add and Configure a Terminate Shape

Next, you'll add and configure a Terminate shape, as follows:

1. Drag a Terminate shape from the Toolbox onto the Orchestration Design Surface beneath the Else shape. Your screen should resemble Figure 2-16.

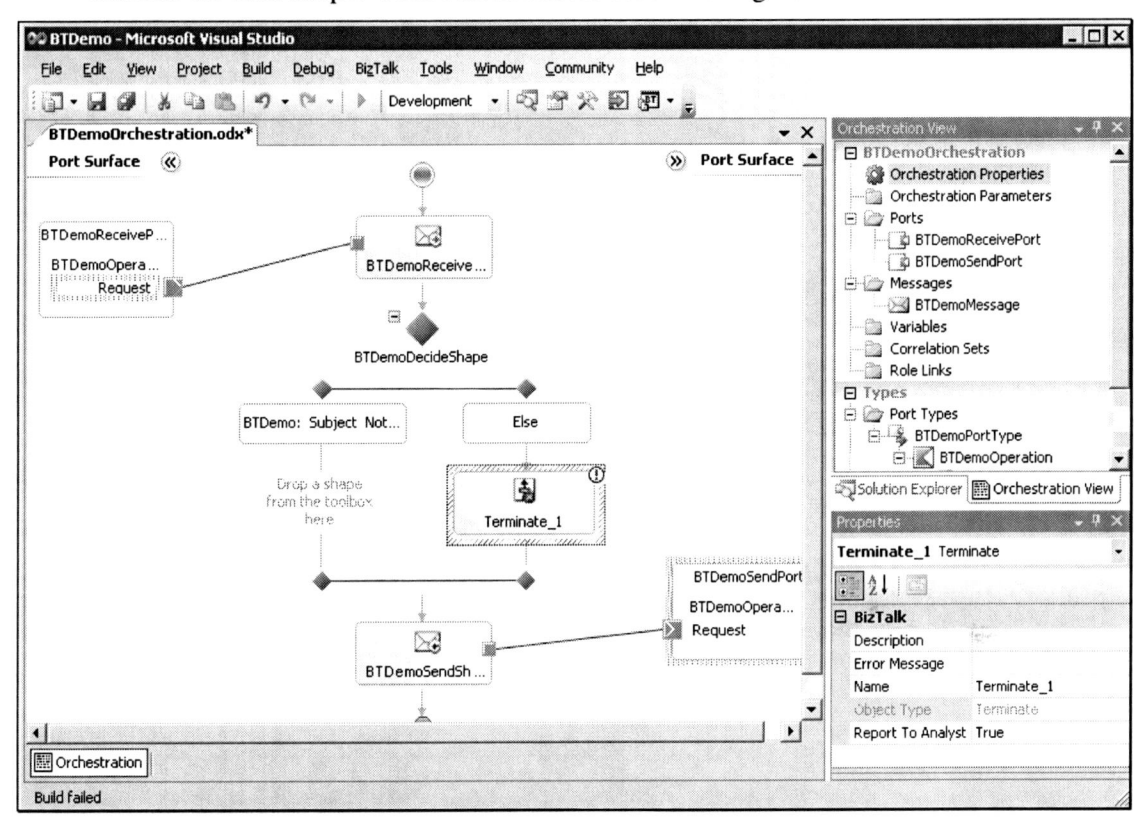

Figure 2-16. Adding a Terminate shape to the orchestration

2. Configure the Terminate shape as follows:

Property	Value
Error Message	"Process terminated due to blank subject";
Name	BTDemoTerminateShape

Loftin

3. Drag BTDemoSendShape to a point that is under the BTDemo: Subject Not Blank rule. Your screen should look like Figure 2-17.

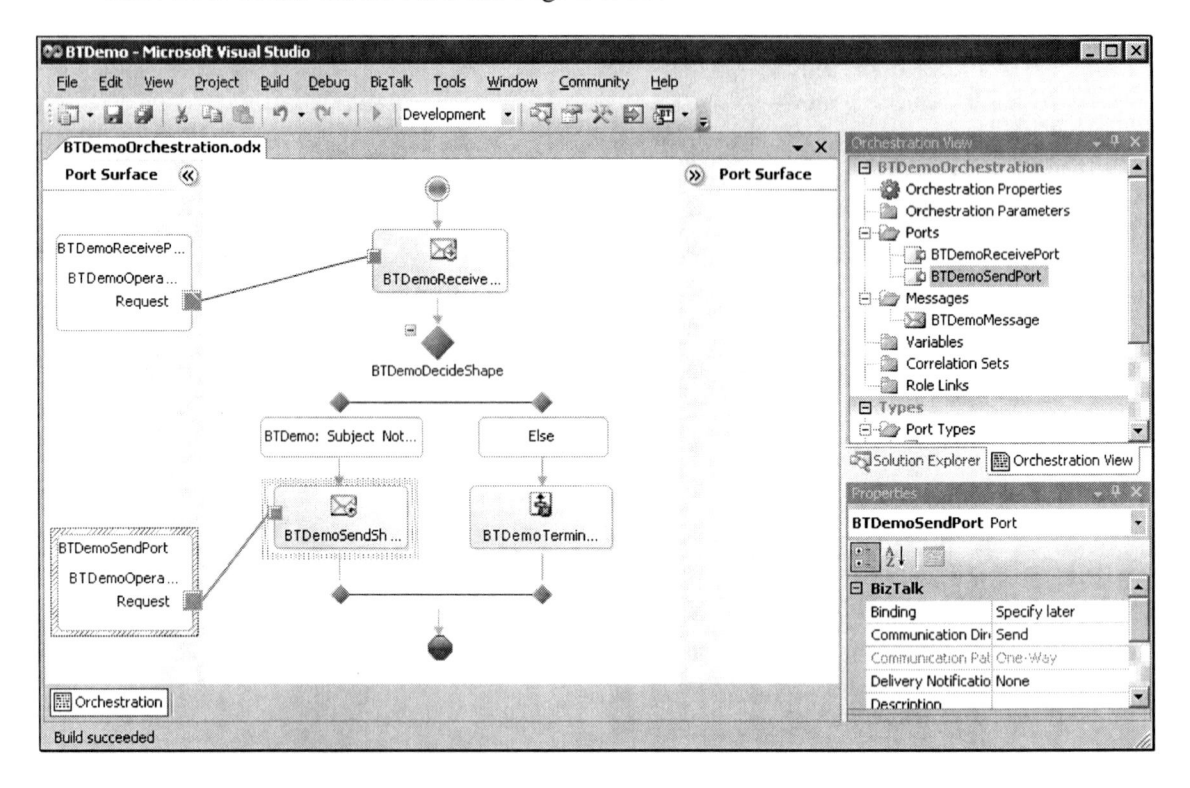

Figure 2-17. Completed Phase 2 orchestration

Note ➡ The BTDemoTerminateShape object would not be necessary just to stop the orchestration, because the orchestration would stop on its own once the Else branch was followed. However, BTDemoTerminateShape records an error message in the log.

Deploy the Project

Finally, follow these steps to deploy the project:

1. Save your project.
2. Using the BizTalk Administration console, bring the BTDemo application to a full stop.
3. Stop and then restart the BizTalk Service BizTalk Group : BizTalkServerApplication Windows service.
4. Deploy your application to the BizTalk server. Close the project after successful deployment.

BizTalk Server Administration Console Tasks

The tasks that you will perform using the BizTalk Server Administration console are detailed in the sections that follow.

Launch the BizTalk Server Administration Console

First, you'll launch the Administration console:

1. Open the BizTalk Server Administration console and navigate to the BizTalk group that is hosting your project.
2. Refresh the BizTalk group by right-clicking the BizTalk Group node and selecting the Refresh menu option.

Review the Receive Location and Send Port Configurations

The tasks that you will be asked to perform in this phase assume that you are using the File Copy example from Phase 1. Therefore, if necessary, reconfigure your receive location and send port to match that of Phase 1. If you are not currently using the File Copy example's settings, review the previous phase for instructions on how to configure the receive location and the send port.

If you have to change the configuration, stop the BTDemo application (full stop), and then restart it. These operations are available by right-clicking the BTDemo application.

Change the Receive Location Pipeline

Follow these steps to change the receive location pipeline:

1. Stop the BTDemo application by right-clicking the BTDemo application node and selecting Stop.

2. Select the Partial Stop option and then click the Stop button.

3. Change the pipeline of the receive location from Pass Thru Receive to XML Receive and click the OK button.

Note ➡ In Phase 1, you used the Pass Thru Receive pipeline for the receive location. However, now that you want to examine the contents of the incoming XML message, you need to use the XML Receive pipeline.

4. Start the BTDemo application.

Test Your Application

Follow these steps to test your application:

1. Make a copy of the generated schema instance file. Update it to include information in the subject node. The update contents should resemble the following:

```
<ns0:emailservice xmlns:ns0="http://BTDemo.BTDemoEmailSchema">
  <transx command="command_0" datetime="datetime_1" />
  <send>
   <fromaddr />
   <toaddr />
   <cc />
   <bcc />
   <subject>This is a test</subject>
   <body />
   <bodyformat />
   <attachments>
    <attachment filename="filename_0" />
   </attachments>
  </send>
</ns0:emailservice>
```

2. Copy the updated instance file to the receive location. The BTDemo application should copy the file to the output location specified by the send port.

3. Copy the original instance file to the receive location. It should *not* be copied to the output location because of the rule. However, it should disappear from the receive location and an error message should be generated.

The orchestration you created as part of the earlier "Add and Configure a Terminate Shape" section in this phase was designed to terminate with an error message if the subject was blank. The following task confirms that the application did terminate and that an error message was generated.

Use the Health and Activity Tracking Tool

Follow these steps to use the BizTalk Health and Activity Tracking tool:

1. Launch the Health and Activity Tracking (HAT) tool (see Figure 2-18).

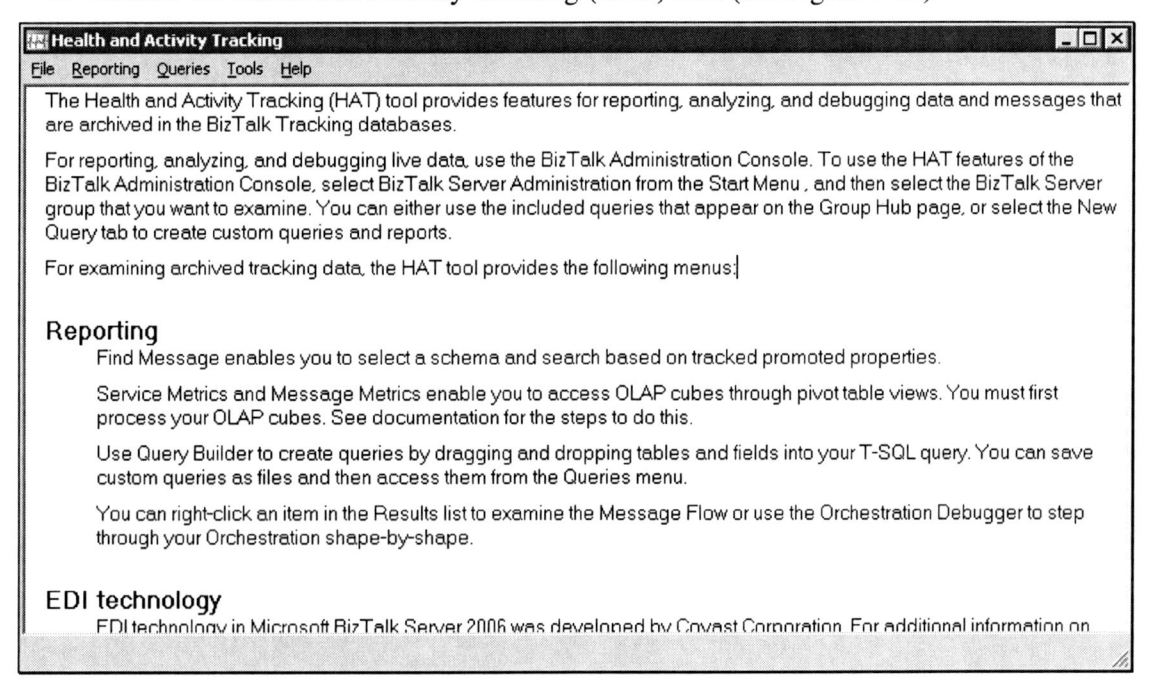

Figure 2-18. The Health and Activity Tracking tool

2. Select Reporting ➤ Find Message. The Find Message View dialog box shown in Figure 2-19 displays.

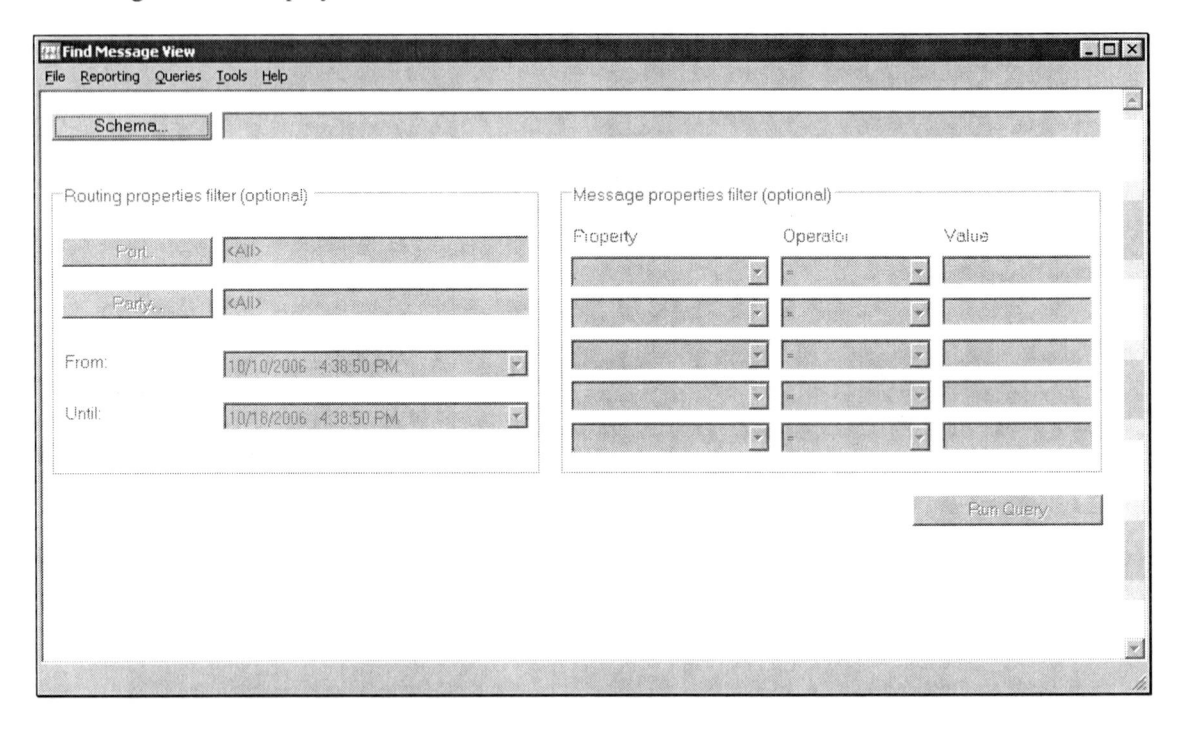

Figure 2-18. Find Message View dialog box

3. Click the Schema button and select the http://BTDemo.BTDemoEmailSchema#emailservice schema.

4. Click the Run Query button. The bottom of your screen will be populated with data. If you are the only person on the server, your message will be at the top of the list; otherwise, you will have to hunt for it. Your screen should resemble Figure 2-19.

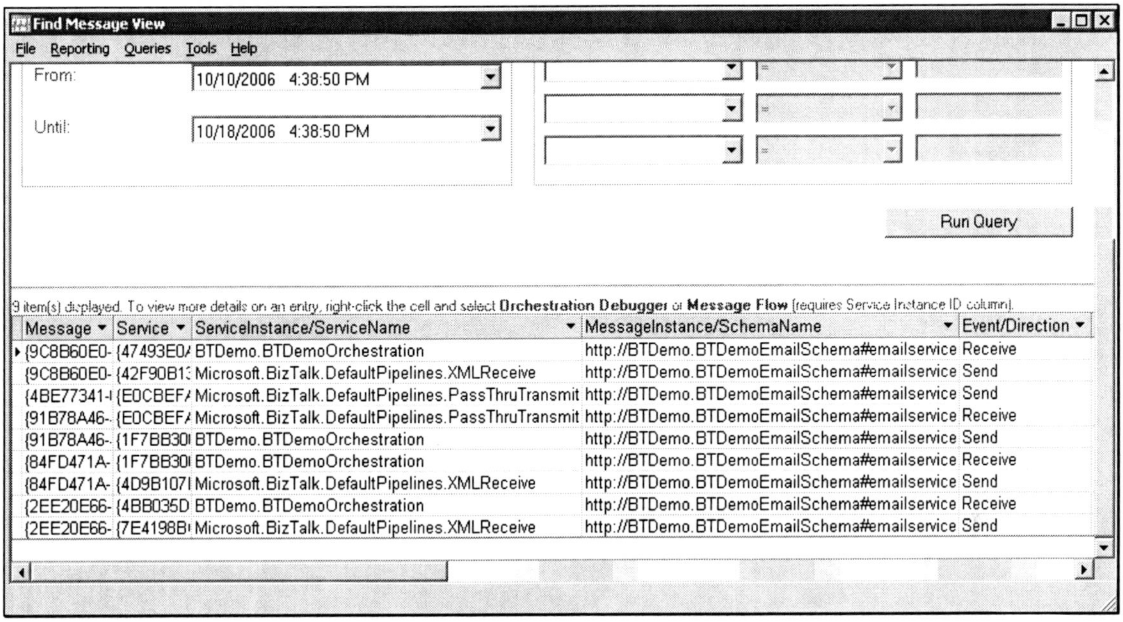

Figure 2-19. Query results

5. Right-click the row that contains BTDdemo.BTDemoOrchestration in the ServiceInstance/ServiceName column and select the Message Flow menu option. Your screen should now look like Figure 2-20.

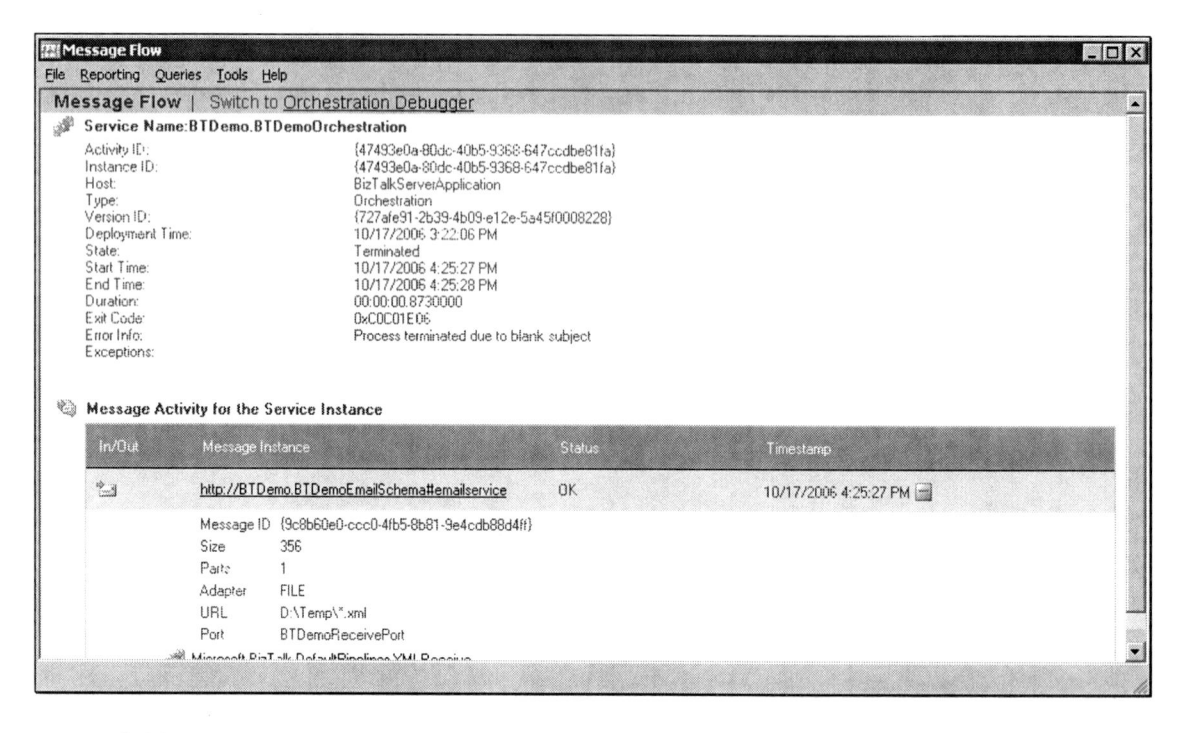

Figure 2-20. Message flow detail

Note that the State of the orchestration is Terminated and that the Error Info is "Process terminated due to blank subject."

HAT has another tool, "Most recent 100 services terminated with errors," that you can use to discover information about the terminated orchestration, as follows:

1. Select Queries ➤ Most Recent 100 Services Terminated with Errors. Your screen should resemble Figure 2-21.

firstPress: Working with Schemas

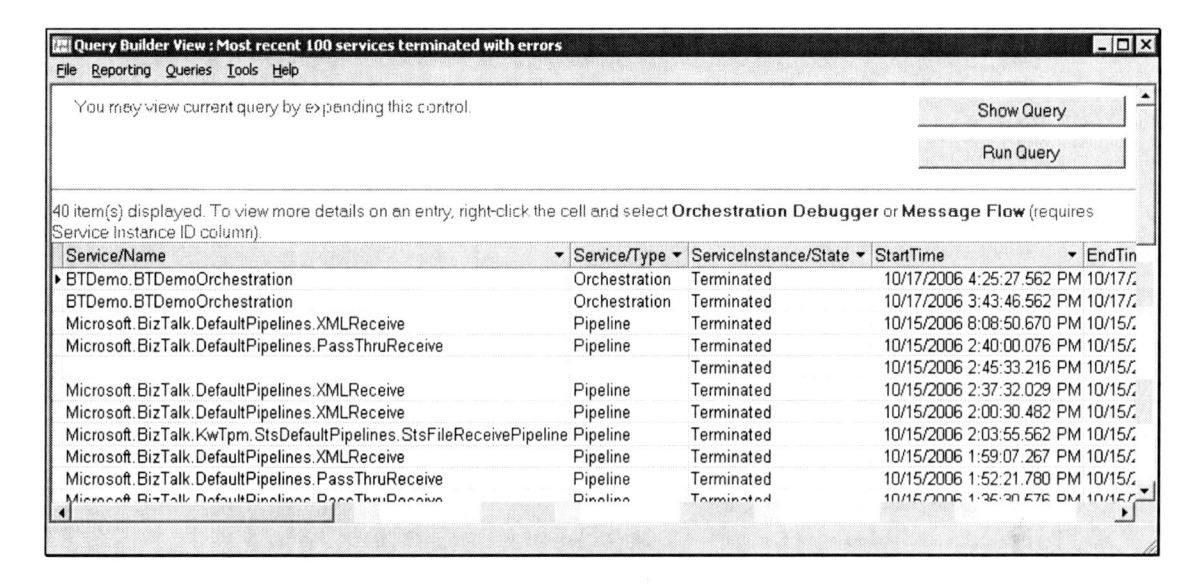

Figure 2-21. Query results: Most recent 100 services terminated with errors

2. Click the Show Query button.

3. Modify the SQL query as follows (changes are shown in bold font):

-- Copyright (c) Microsoft Corporation. All rights reserved.
--
-- THIS CODE AND INFORMATION IS PROVIDED "AS IS" WITHOUT WARRANTY OF ANY KIND,
-- WHETHER EXPRESSED OR IMPLIED, INCLUDING BUT NOT LIMITED TO THE IMPLIED
-- WARRANTIES OF MERCHANTABILITY AND/OR FITNESS FOR A PARTICULAR PURPOSE.
-- THE ENTIRE RISK OF USE OR RESULTS IN CONNECTION WITH THE USE OF THIS CODE
-- AND INFORMATION REMAINS WITH THE USER.

-- Retrieve last 100 service instances that terminated with an error
-- Note: Joins are used for localized strings only
SELECT top 100
       [Service/Name], [Service/Type],
       [ServiceInstance/State],
       dateadd(minute, @UtcOffsetMin, [ServiceInstance/StartTime]) as [StartTime], -- can't use 'as [ServiceInstance/StartTime]' since this prevents SQL from using index on that column (conflicts with ORDER BY)

dateadd(minute, @UtcOffsetMin, [ServiceInstance/EndTime]) as [EndTime], -- can't use 'as [ServiceInstance/EndTime]' since this prevents SQL from using index on that column (conflicts with ORDER BY)
    [ServiceInstance/Duration],
    [ServiceInstance/ExitCode],
    [ServiceInstance/ErrorInfo],
    [ServiceInstance/Host],
    [Service/AssemblyName],
    [ServiceInstance/InstanceID],
    [ServiceInstance/ActivityID],
    [Service/ServiceGUID],
    [Service/ServiceClassGUID]
FROM dbo.dtav_ServiceFacts sf WITH (READPAST)
JOIN dbo.dta_ServiceState st WITH (READPAST) ON st.strState = sf.[ServiceInstance/State]
-- Terminated = 3, also check for non-zero ExitCode
WHERE ((st.nServiceStateId = 3) OR (0!= sf.[ServiceInstance/ExitCode]))
  and [Service/Name] = 'BTDemo.BTDemoOrchestration'
ORDER BY sf.[ServiceInstance/EndTime] desc

4. Click the Run Query button. Your screen should look like Figure 2-22.

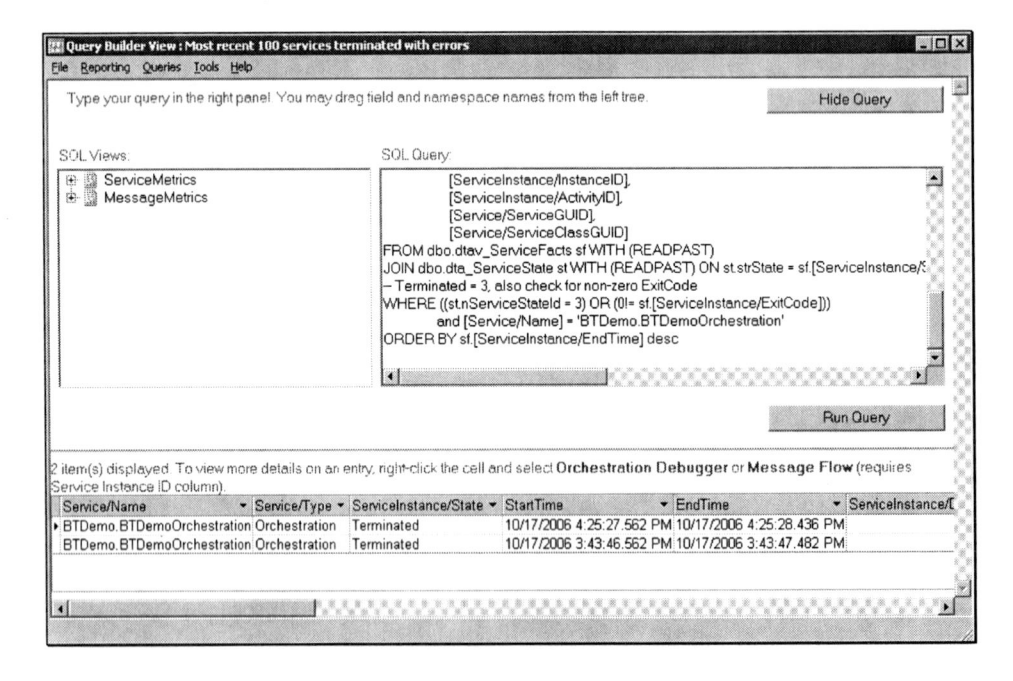

Figure 2-22. Modified query results

If you scroll your screen to the right, under the column ServiceInstance/ErrorInfo you will notice the error message "Process terminated due to blank subject."

5. Close HAT.

6. Bring the BTDemo application to a full stop.

7. Close the BizTalk Administration console.

Summary

This phase introduced more complexity into your BizTalk project. It introduced you to schemas, Decide and Terminate shapes, and the HAT tool. Before moving on to Phase 3, let's review what you learned in this phase:

- Schemas are used to define the structure and content of messages. They are one of the four file types that can be defined for a BizTalk project: orchestration, map, pipeline, or schema.

- Three different types of schemas can be defined: flat file, property, and regular (i.e., schema).

- Schemas can be used to validate that incoming messages are properly formatted, in orchestrations to make decisions about the content of messages that conform to the schema, and to generate instance messages that conform to the schema. The instance messages can be used for test purposes or as examples provided to development teams to demonstrate the types of messages your BizTalk project can handle. Also, schema validation can be used to verify that you have properly designed the schema to represent the files of existing applications.

- One way of making data in a message available to an orchestration is by promoting a node or nodes within the schema that represents the data.

- A Decide shape is a BizTalk graphical object that is used to implement IF-THEN-ELSE programming logic in an orchestration.

- A Terminate shape is a BizTalk graphical object that is used to programmatically terminate a BizTalk orchestration.

- The Health and Activity Tracking (HAT) tool provides features for reporting, analyzing, and debugging data and messages that are archived in the BizTalk tracking databases.

PHASE 3

Message Mapping

In this phase, you will modify the BTDemo project of Phase 2 to add a flat-file schema. Also, instead of writing a termination error message when the <subject> node of the incoming message is blank, you will map the contents of the incoming message to a new message that has a flat-file format, and you will then write the flat-file message to a different send port.

Note ➡ This phase takes approximately one hour and fifteen minutes to complete.

Visual Studio 2005 Tasks

The tasks that you will perform using Visual Studio 2005 are covered in detail in the sections that follow.

Add a Flat-File Schema to the Project

As you saw in Phase 2, schemas are used to define the format of XML messages. Schemas are also used to define the format of flat files. However, instead of using a schema file, we must use a flat-file schema file to define the format of a flat file.

1. Open the BTDemo project
2. Add a new item to the project.
3. Select the Flat File Schema option and name the schema **BTDemoFlatFileSchema.xsd**. Your screen should resemble Figure 3-1.

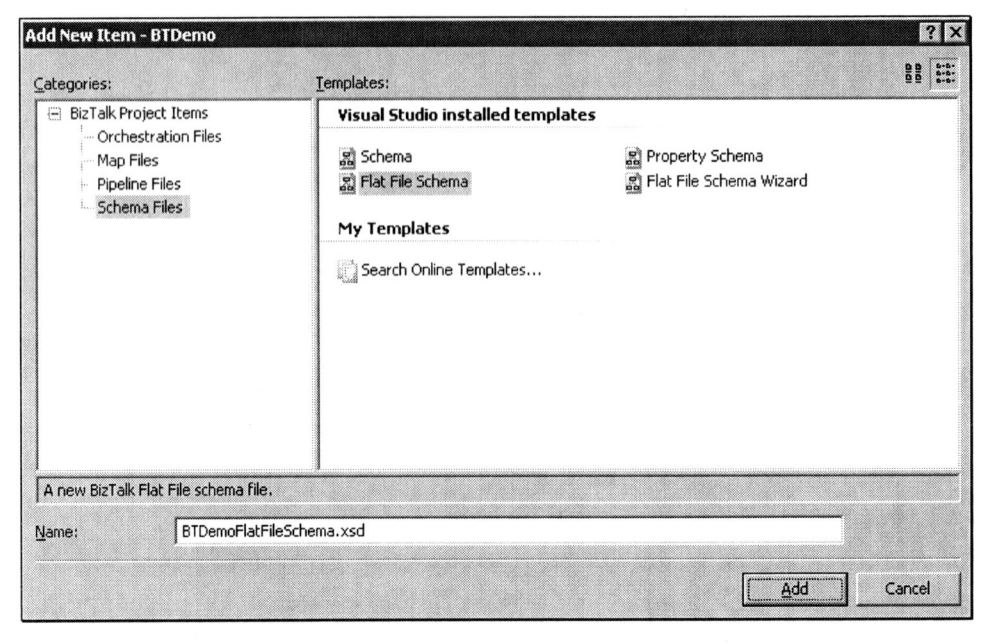

Figure 3-1. Selecting a flat-file schema template

4. Click the Add button.

5. Rename the root node of the schema to be **EmailService**.

6. Similar to what you did in Phase 2, define child field attribute nodes of the schema. Those nodes and the properties to be assigned to them are shown in the following table.

Node Name	Minimum Length with Pad Character Property
DateTime	32
FromAddr	64
ToAddr	64
Cc	128
Bcc	128
Subject	256
Body	512
BodyFormat	64

firstPress: Message Mapping 61

Even though you are creating a flat file, the schema that defines it will always be in XML format. Also, your schema must still have a root node. You have named the root node EmailService.

Note ➡ All of the records in the flat file that you are creating will be of the same format. That is why the nodes that you are creating are *child field attributes* of the root node. However, if the flat file contained different record types, such as orders and their order details, order detail records would be created in the schema as child records of the root node.

When you are done, your screen should look like Figure 3-2.

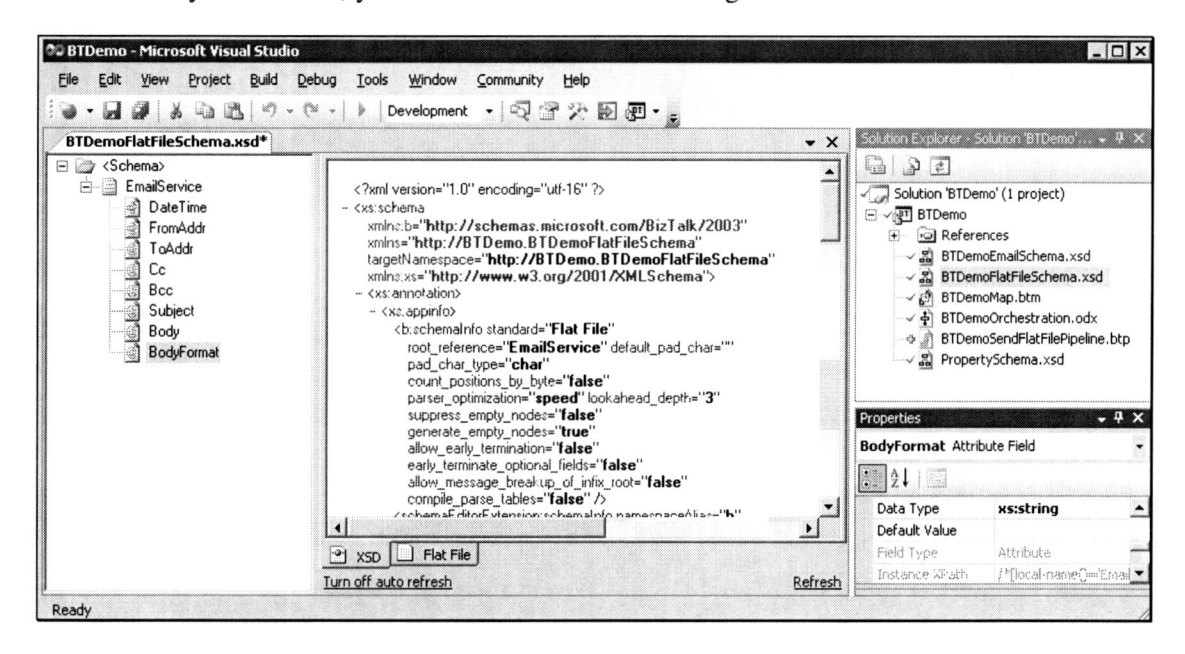

Figure 3-2. Completed flat-file schema definition

7. As you did in Phase 2, validate the schema and generate an instance file. When you work with flat files, the instance file can be created in a *flat file* or an *XML format*. The format is controlled by setting the Generate Instance Output Type property in the property page of the flat-file schema to Native or XML, respectively.

8. Save the project.

Loftin

Map Fields from the Input Message to the New Message

Because you are transferring data from records of one format to records of another, fields in the input message must be individually mapped to fields in the output record. To do this, you must create a map file.

1. Add a map file to your project and name it **BTDemoMap.btm**. Your screen should resemble Figure 3-3.

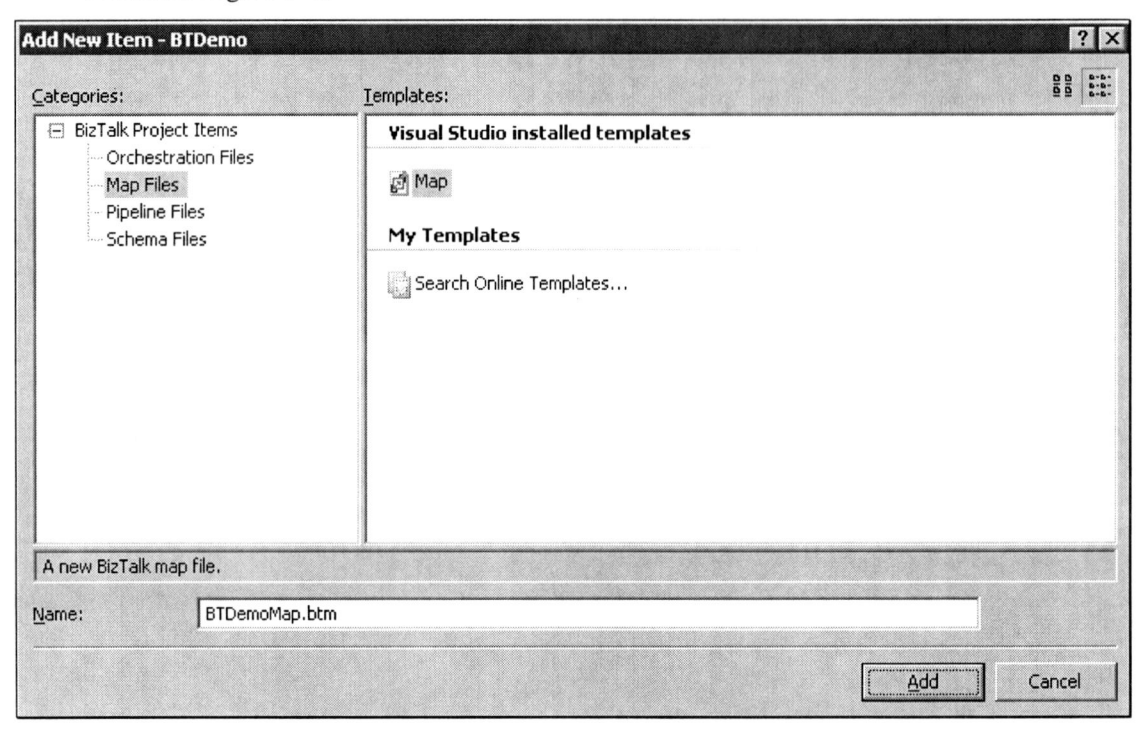

Figure 3-3. Selecting a map template

2. Click the Add button. Your screen should now look like Figure 3-4.

firstPress: Message Mapping 63

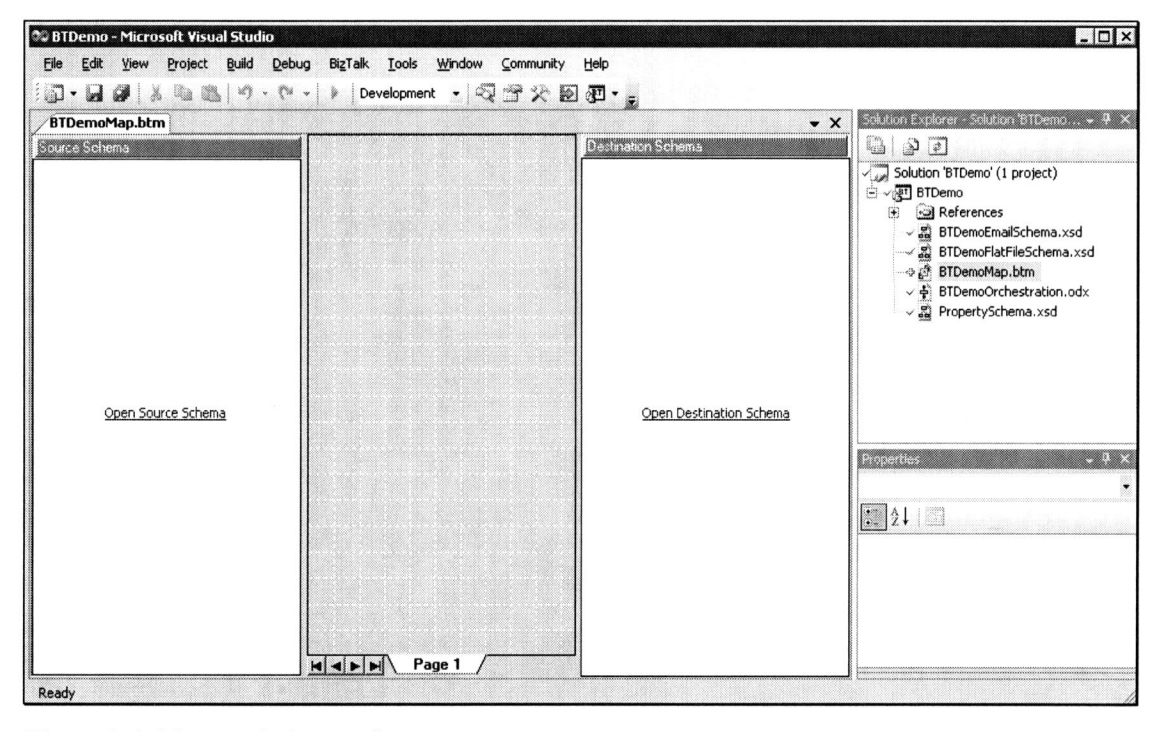

Figure 3-4. Mapper design surface

3. Open the Source and Destination Schemas. You will be using BTDemoEmailSchema as your source and BTDemoFlatFileSchema as your destination.
4. Drag and drop the similarly named fields in the Source Schema to fields of the Destination Schema as per the following table.

Source Schema	Destination Schema
datetime	DateTime
fromaddr	FromAddr
toaddr	ToAddr
cc	Cc
bcc	Bcc
subject	Subject
body	Body
bodyformat	BodyFormat

Loftin

When you finish, your screen should look like Figure 3-5.

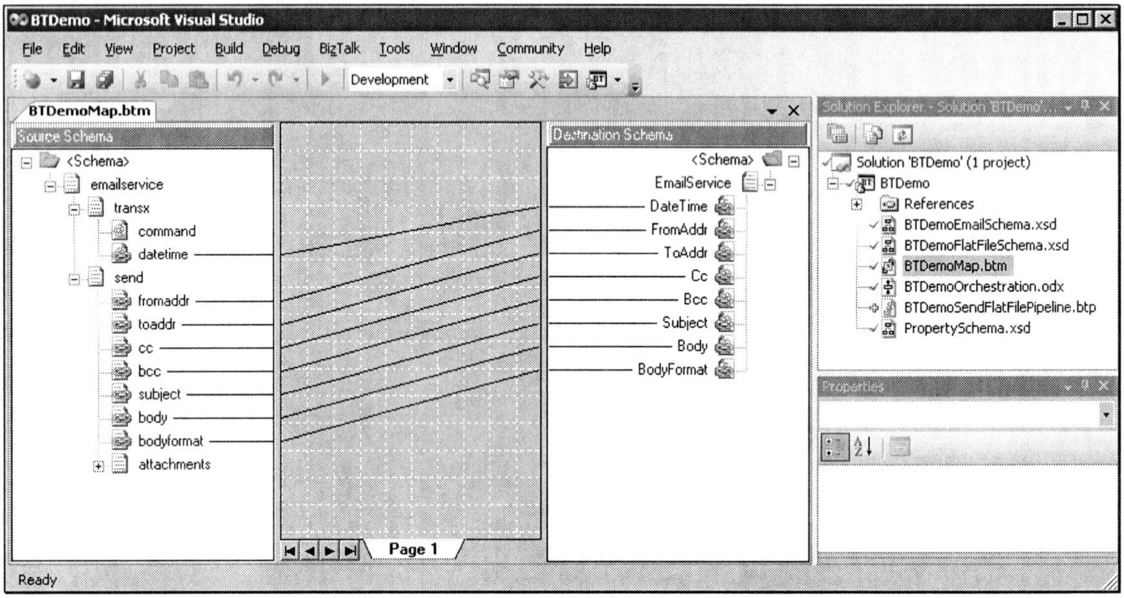

Figure 3-5. Completed message map

Validate the Map

Once you have created a map, you should validate it to ensure that it is accurate and can be processed successfully by the BizTalk server. It is better to debug an application at design time than at runtime.

1. Make a copy of the instance file generated by the BTDemoEmailMessageSchema that was generated as part of Phase 2. Revise it to remove the data assigned to the fields. The revised copy of the instance file should resemble the following:

```
<ns0:emailservice xmlns:ns0="http://BTDemo.BTDemoEmailSchema">
 <transx command="" datetime="" />
 <send>
  <fromaddr />
  <toaddr />
  <cc />
  <bcc />
  <subject />
```

```
  <body />
  <bodyformat />
  <attachments>
    <attachment filename="" />
  </attachments>
 </send>
</ns0:emailservice>
```

2. Open the property page for the BTDemoMap.btm node (see Figure 3-6).

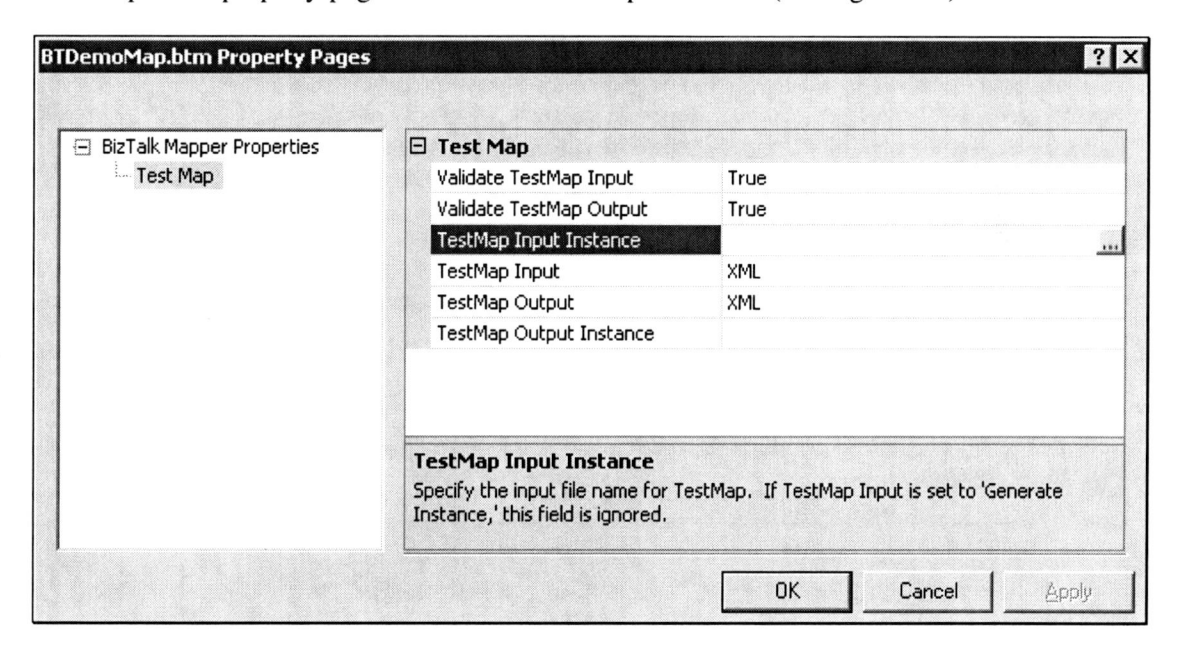

Figure 3-6. Specifying the message file to map

3. Set the TestMap Input Instance to point to the revised instance file created from the BTDemoEmailMessageSchema, which was created in step 1.

4. Validate the map by right-clicking the BTDemoMap.btm node in Solution Explorer and selecting the Validate menu option. You should get the message "Component invocation succeeded" in the Output window.

Test the Map

You should test the map to ensure that it is performing as designed. The test will attempt to map the fields in the Source instance document to the Destination instance document.

1. Test the map by right-clicking the BTDemoMap.btm node and selecting the Test Map menu option. The results you see in the Output window should resemble the following:

Invoking component...
Test Map used the following file: <file:///F:\Program Files\Microsoft BizTalk Server 2006\Projects\BTDemo\Copy (3) of BTDemoMailMsg.xml> as input to the map.
Test Map success for map file F:\Program Files\Microsoft BizTalk Server 2006\Projects\BTDemo\BTDemo\BTDemoMap.btm. The output is stored in the following file: <file:///D:\Documents and Settings\rloftin\Local Settings\Temp\2_MapData\BTDemoMap_output.xml>
Component invocation succeeded.

Note ➡ The Test Map function can generate a test map output file in an XML or Native format, and is controlled by the Test Map Output property on the BTDemoMap property page. Accept the default (XML) Test Map Output property.

When performing an enterprise application integration (EAI) with existing systems that can provide you with test files, the ability to test proper execution of your BizTalk application during design time will prove to be valuable.

2. View the contents of the Test Map Output file.

3. Save the project.

Modify the Orchestration

Next, you'll modify the orchestration as follows:

1. Open BTDemoOrchestration.
2. Switch to Orchestration View.

3. Add a new message. Configure it as follows:

Property	Value
Identifier	BTDemoFlatFileMessage
Message Type	Schemas ➤ BTDemo.BTDemoFlatFileSchema

4. Delete BTDemoTerminateShape.

Add a Transform Shape

As its name implies, a Transform shape is used to transform a message from one format to another.

1. Add a Transform shape to the orchestration under the Else shape. Your screen should look like Figure 3-7.

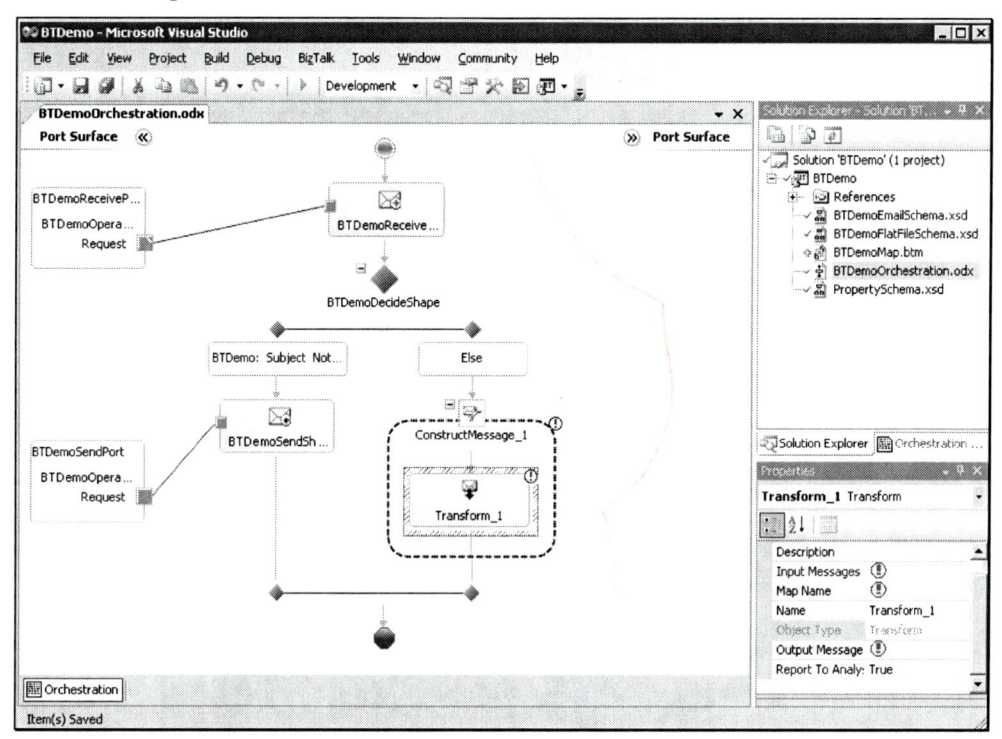

Figure 3-7. Orchestration Design Surface with a Transform shape

2. Double-click the Transform_1 shape. Your screen should now look like Figure 3-8.

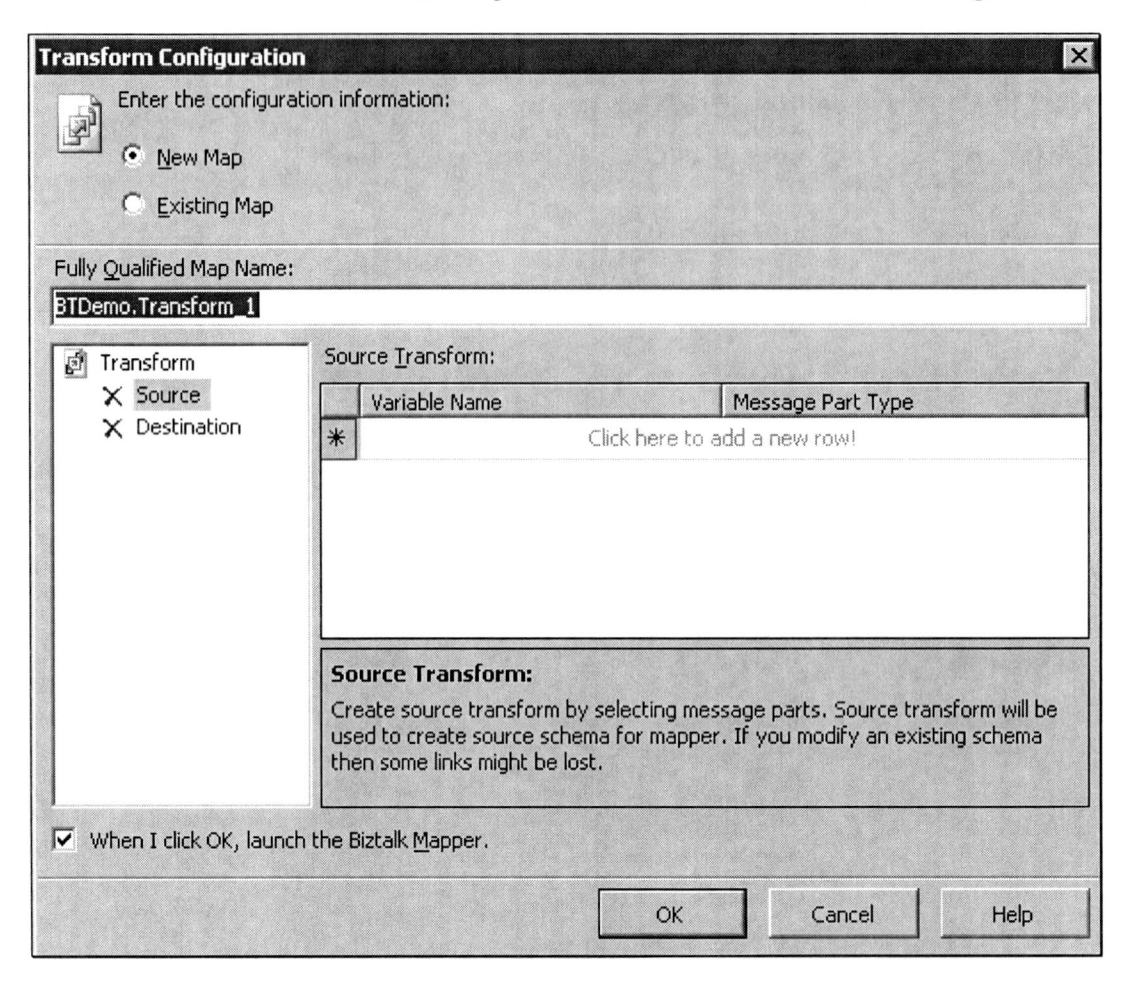

Figure 3-8. Configuring the Transform shape

3. Click the Existing Map option and select the BTDemo.BTDemoMap map file option as the Fully Qualified Map Name.

4. Click the Transform ➤ Source node in the left pane and then select BTDemoMessage as the Variable Name.

5. Click the Transform ➤ Destination node and then select BTDemoFlatFileMessage as the Variable Name. Your screen should resemble Figure 3-9.

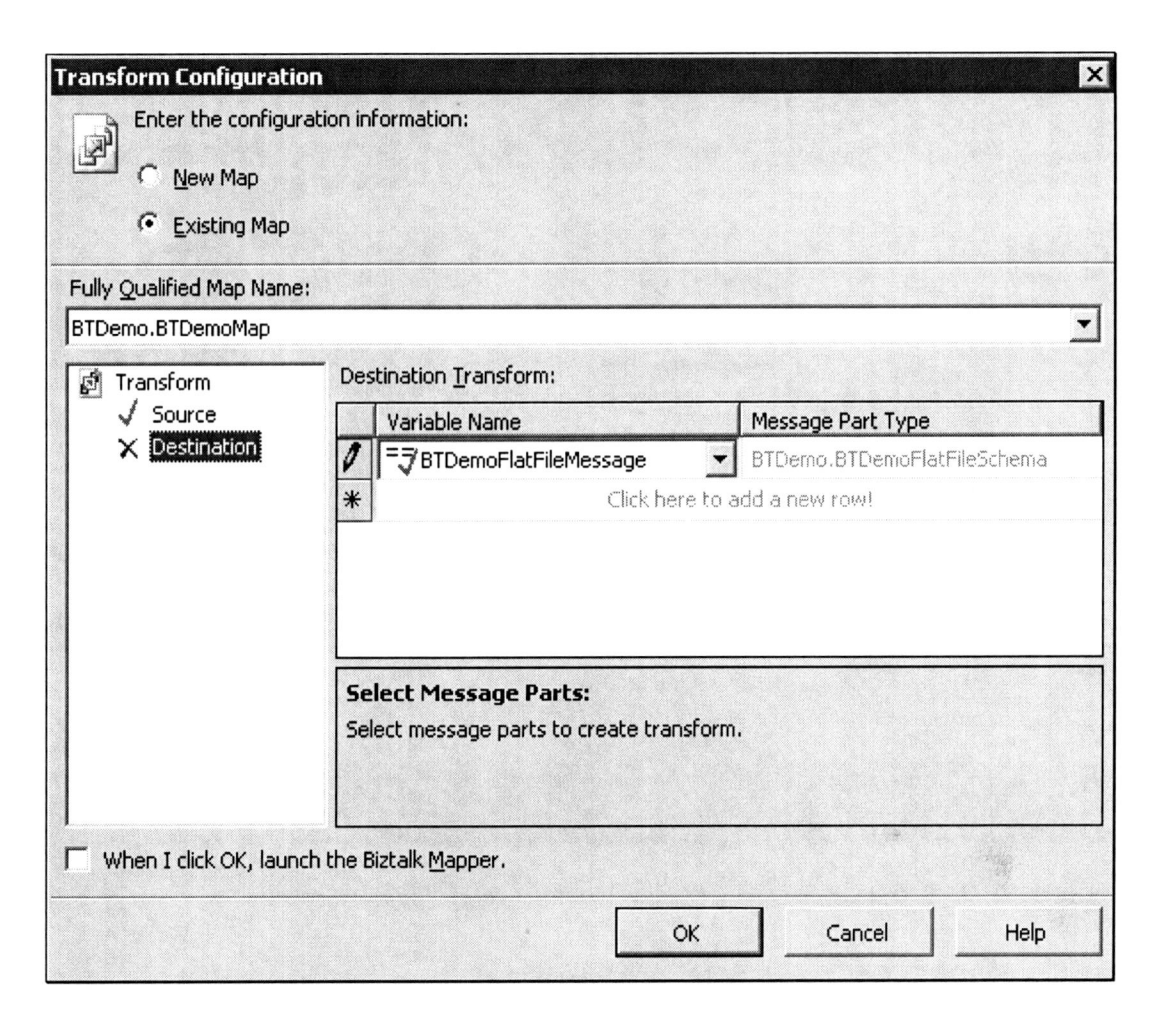

Figure 3-9. Configured Transform shape

6. Click OK.

7. Change the name Transform_1 to **BTDemoTransform**.

8. Change the name ConstructMessage_1 to **BTDemoConstructMessage**. Your screen should now look like Figure 3-10.

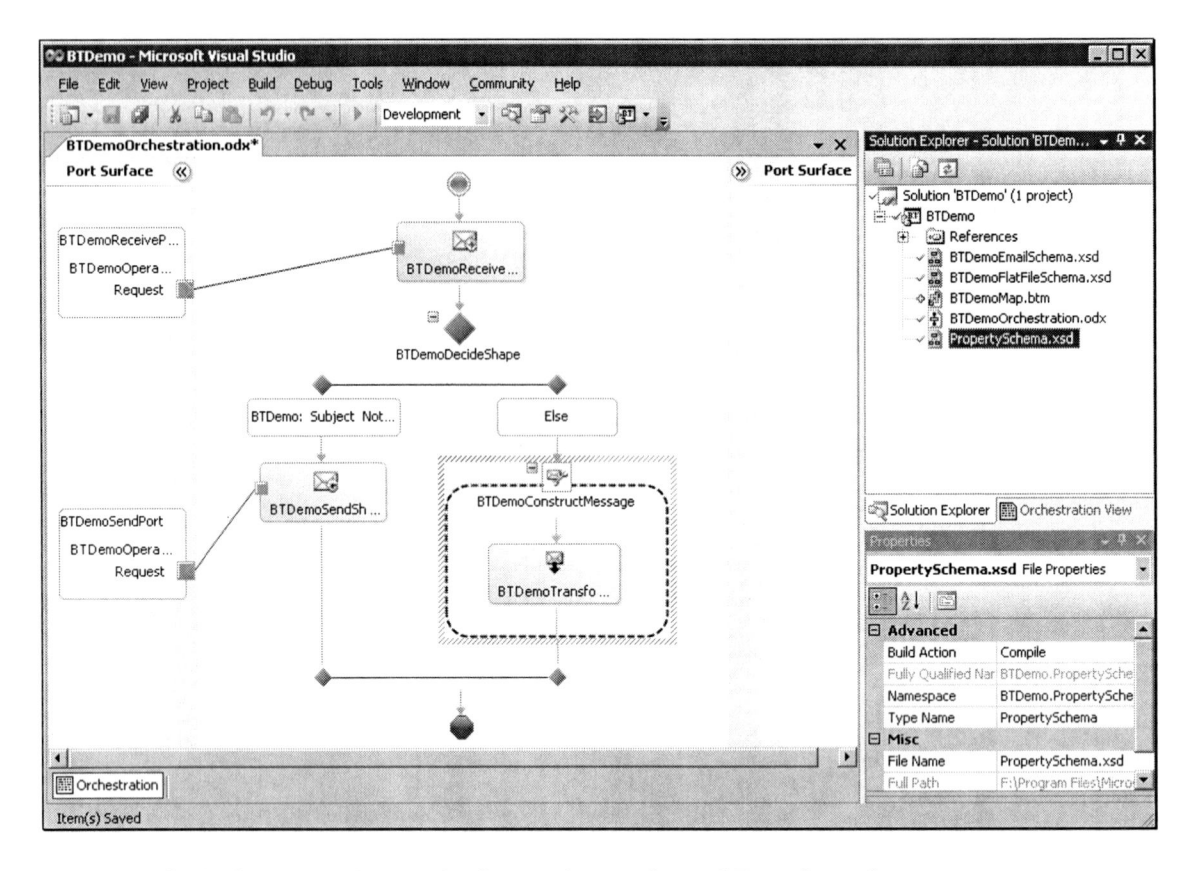

Figure 3-10. Orchestration Design Surface with a configured Transform shape

Add a New Port Type and a New Port

Since we are using a different schema, we need to add a new port type to the orchestration, as follows:

1. As per the instructions in Phase 1, add a *new, one-way* port type. Configure it as follows:

Property	Value to Be Assigned
Identifier	BTDemoFlatFilePortType
Operation ➤ Identifier	BTDemoFlatFileOperation
Request ➤ Message Type	Schemas ➤ BTDemo.BTDemoFlatFileSchema

2. Drag a port shape from the Toolbox to the Port Surface. Configure it as follows:

Property	Value to Be Assigned
Name	BTDemoFlatFilePort
Use an Existing Port Type	BTDemo.BTDemoFlatFilePortType
Port direction of communication	I'll always be sending messages on this port
Port binding	Specify Later

Add a Send Shape

Next, add a Send shape as follows:

1. Drag a Send shape from the Toolbox and place it under the Transform shape. Configure it as follows:

Property	Value to Be Assigned
Name	BTDemoFlatFileSendShape
Message	BTDemoFlatFileMessage
Operation	BTDemoFlatFilePort.BTDemoFlatFileOperation.Request

2. Your screen should resemble Figure 3-11.

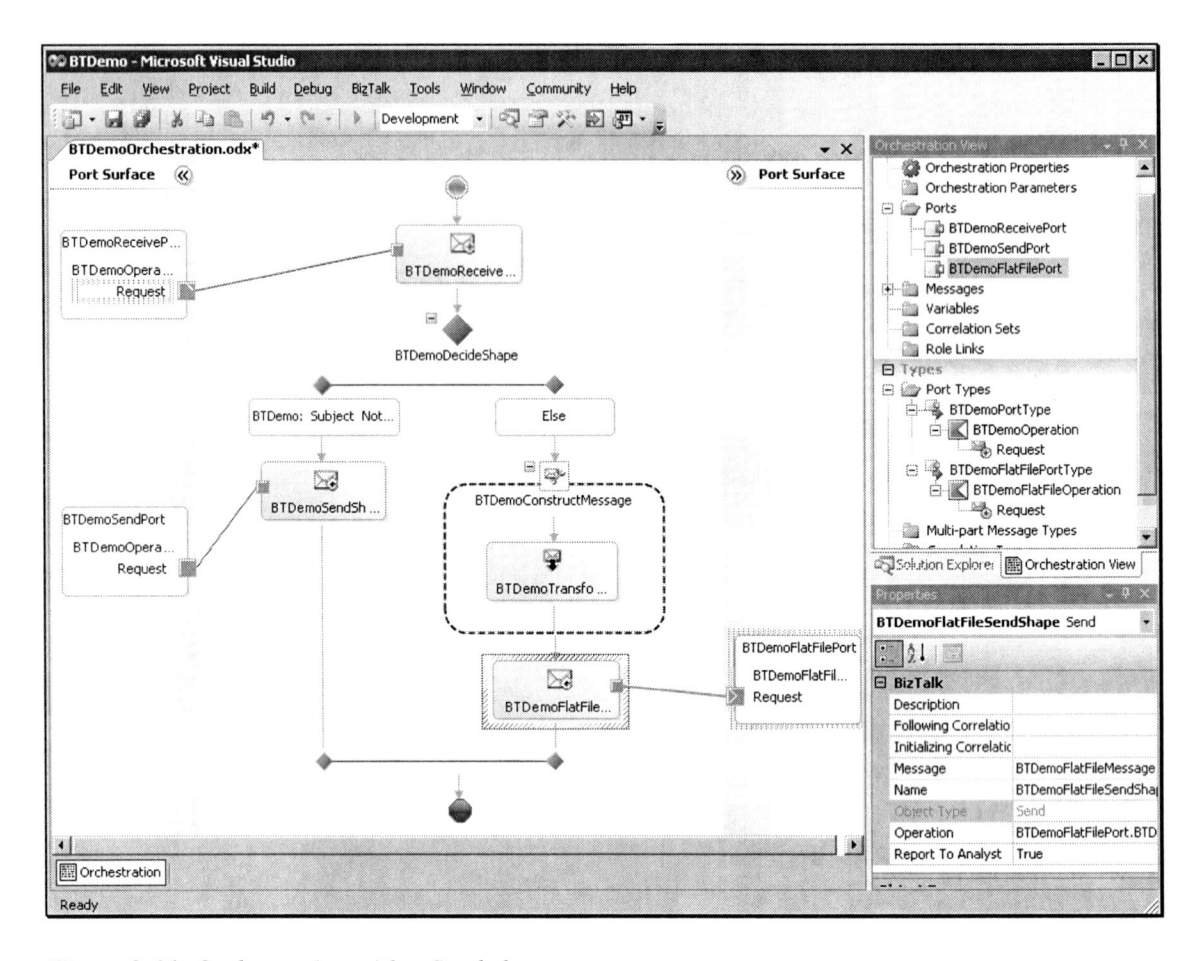

Figure 3-11. Orchestration with a Send shape

3. Save the project.

Add a Send Pipeline

A Send pipeline is needed to *assemble* the information into a flat-file format.

1. Switch to Solution Explorer and add a Send pipeline to the project. Your screen should resemble Figure 3-12.

firstPress: Message Mapping 73

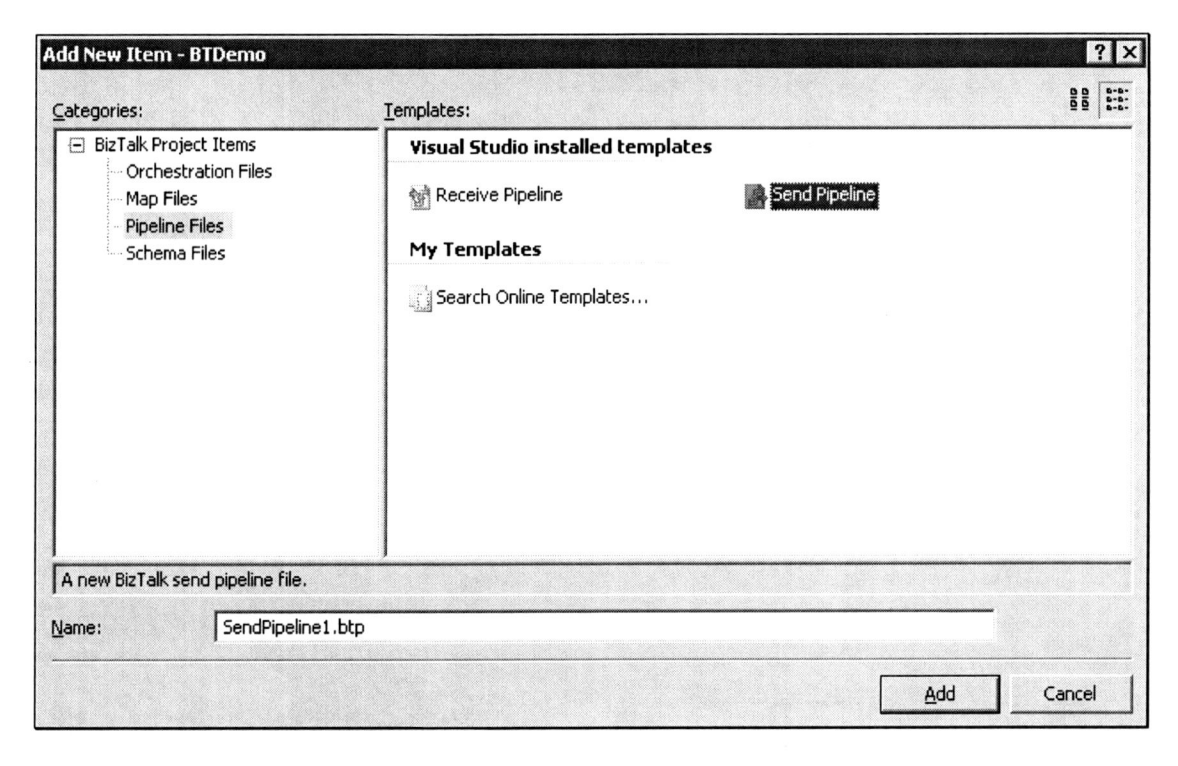

Figure 3-12. Selecting a Send pipeline template

2. Name the pipeline **BTDemoSendFlatFilePipeline.btp** and then click the Add button.

3. Drag the Flat File Assembler shape from the Toolbox and drop it underneath the Assemble artifact on the pipeline design surface, as shown in Figure 3-13.

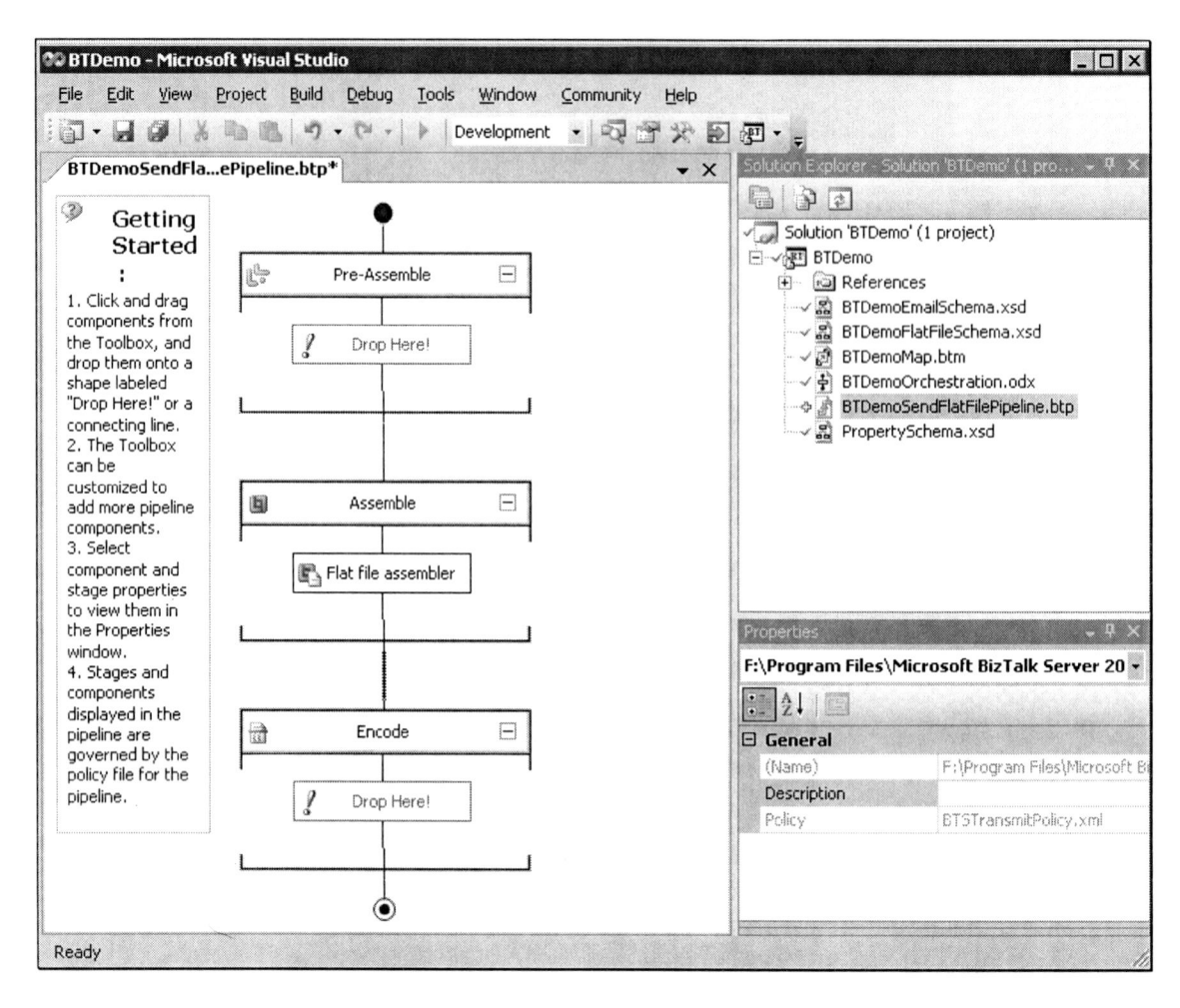

Figure 3-13. Send pipeline design surface

4. Set the Document Schema property of the Flat File Assembler shape to be BTDemo.BTDemoFlatFileSchema.

Deploy the Project

Deploy the project as follows:

1. Save your project.

2. Using the BizTalk Administration console, bring the BTDemo application to a full stop.

3. Stop and then restart the BizTalk Service BizTalk Group : BizTalkServerApplication Windows service.

4. Deploy your application to the BizTalk server. Close the project after successful deployment.

BizTalk Server Administration Console Tasks

The tasks that you will perform using the BizTalk Server Administration console are detailed in the sections that follow.

Launch the BizTalk Server Administration Console

The BizTalk Server Administration console is used to install, configure, and launch your BizTalk project.

1. Open the BizTalk Server Administration console and navigate to the BizTalk group that is hosting your project.

2. Refresh the BizTalk group by right-clicking the BizTalk Group node and selecting the Refresh menu option.

Review the Receive Location and Send Port Configurations

For the purposes of this exercise, your receive location and send port should be configured as they were for Phase 2 of the project. If this is not the case, review the previous lessons for instructions on how to configure the receive location and send port.

If you have to change the configuration of either the receive location or the send port, stop the BTDemo application (full stop) and then restart it. These operations are available by right-clicking the BTDemo application.

Verify that the BTDemo.BTDemoSendFlatFilePipeline pipeline was added to the BTDemo project. Your screen should look like Figure 3-14.

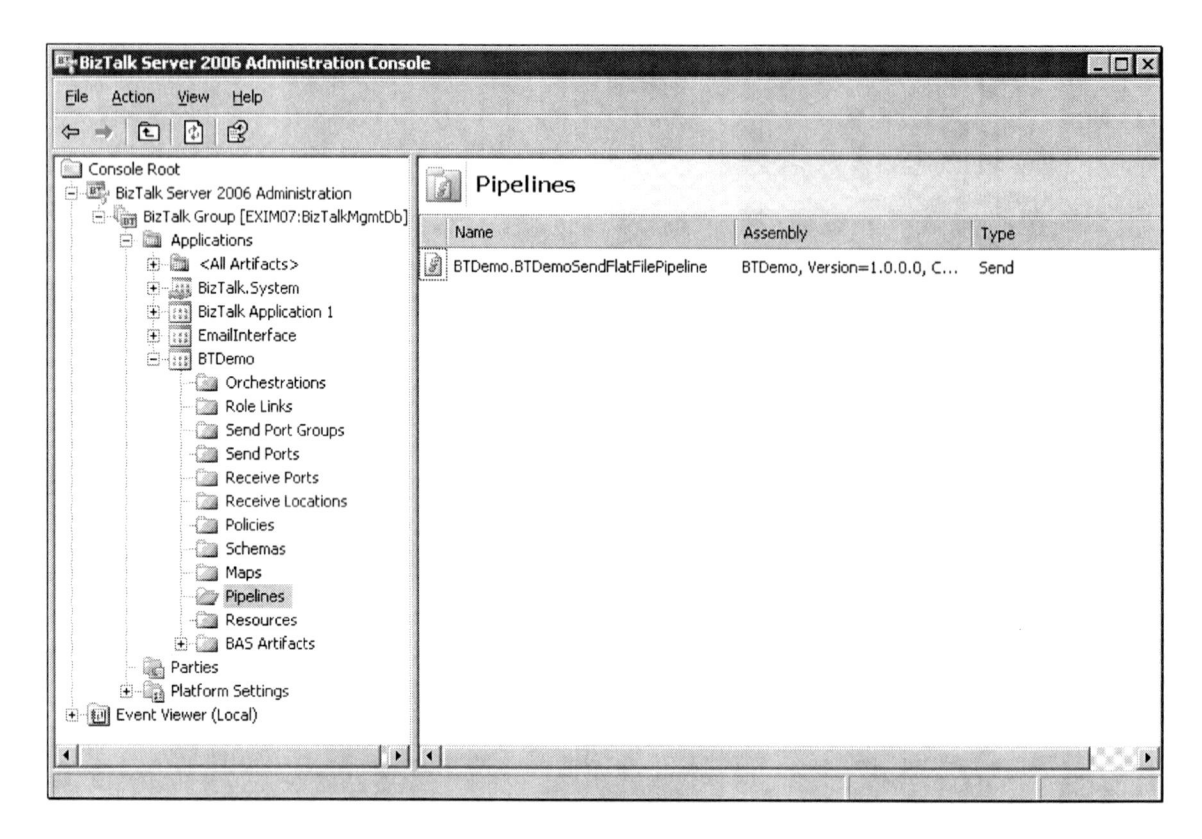

Figure 3-14. BTDemo pipelines

Note ➡ If the BTDemo.BTDemoSendFlatFilePipeline pipeline wasn't added, you may need restart the BizTalk Windows service and redeploy the application.

Add and Configure a Send Port

Follow these steps to add and configure a send port.

1. Add a send port by right-clicking the Send Ports folder and selecting the New ➤ Static One-way Send Port menu option. Your screen should look like Figure 3-15.

firstPress: Message Mapping 77

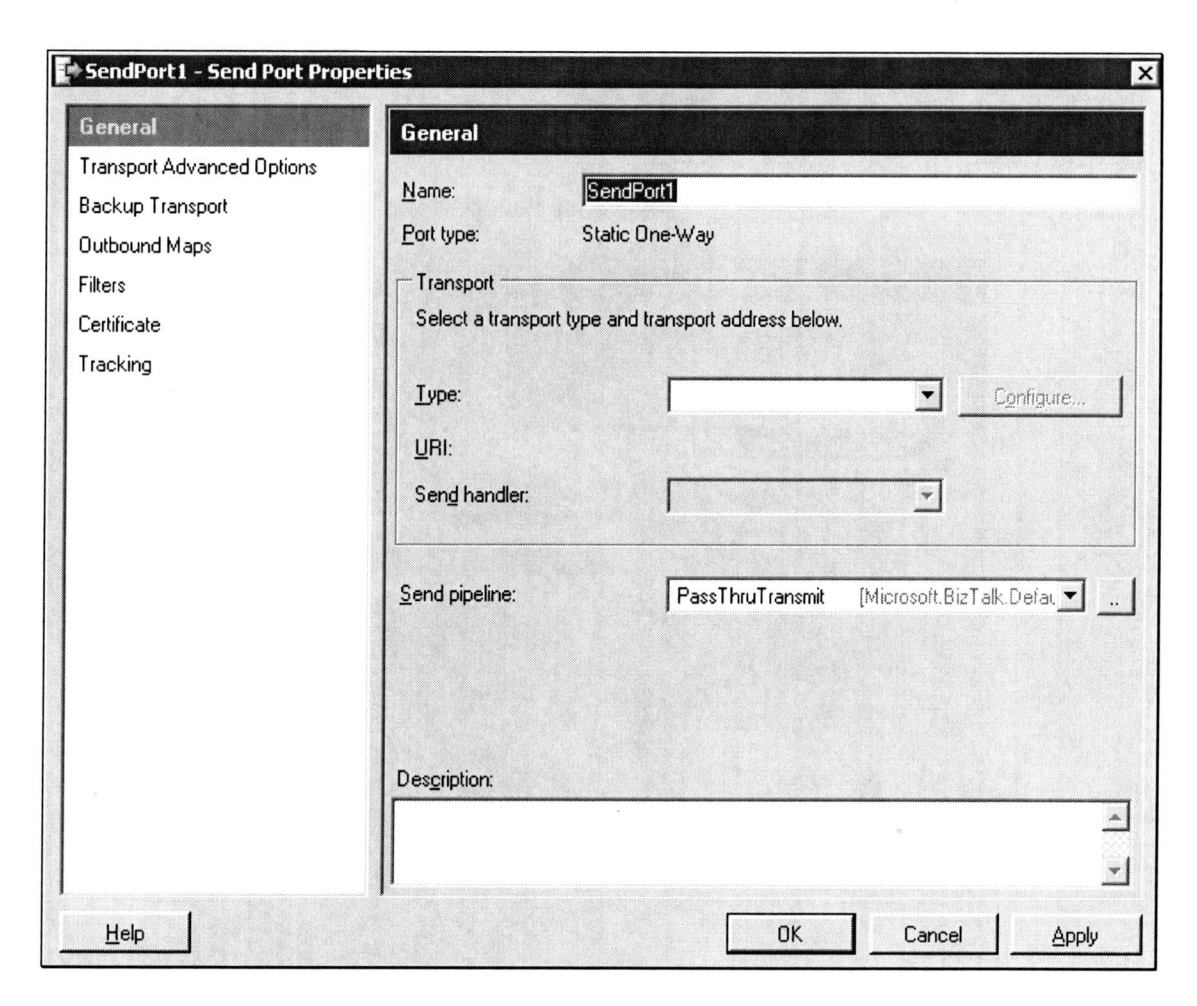

Figure 3-15. Send port configuration

2. Configure the send port as follows:

Property	Value
Name	BTDemoFlatFileSendPort
Transport Type	File
Send pipeline	BTDemo.BTDemoFlatFileSendFlatFilePipeline

> Note → The transport will be configured in the next step.

3. Click the Transport Configure button. Your screen should resemble Figure 3-16.

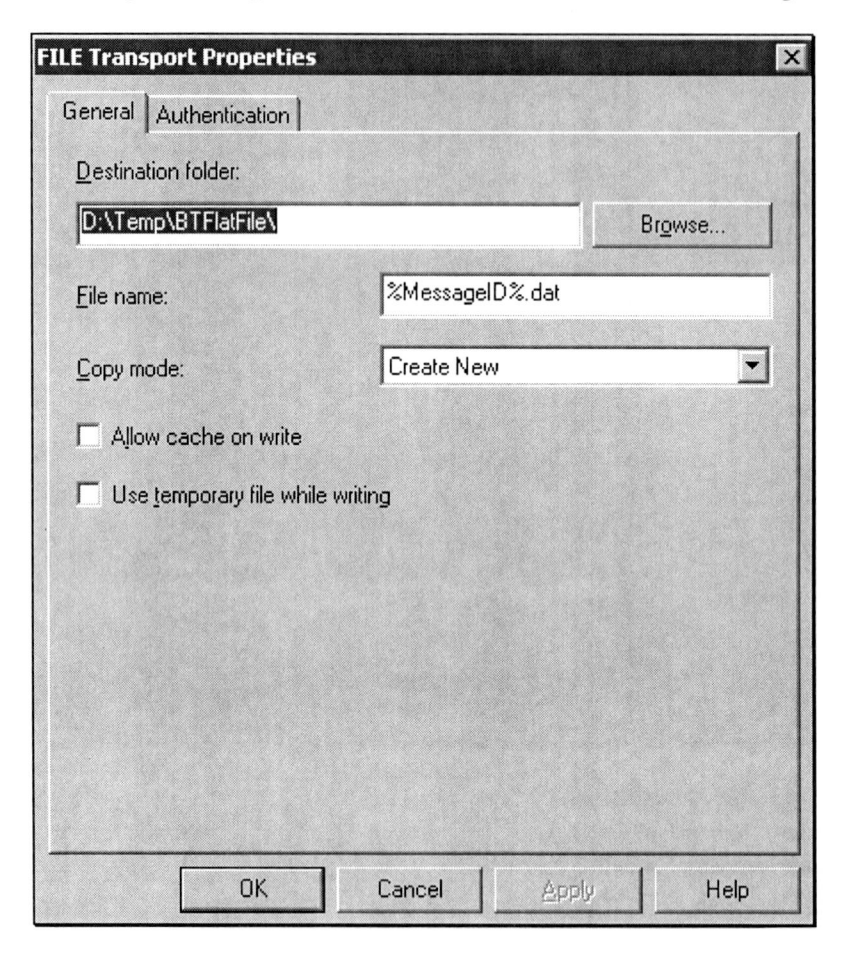

Figure 3-16. File transport configuration

4. Configure the transport as follows and then click the OK button:

Parameter	Value
Destination folder	(*Information appropriate for your installation*)
File name	%MessageID%.txt

5. Click the OK button to close the Send Port Properties dialog box. Your screen should resemble Figure 3-17.

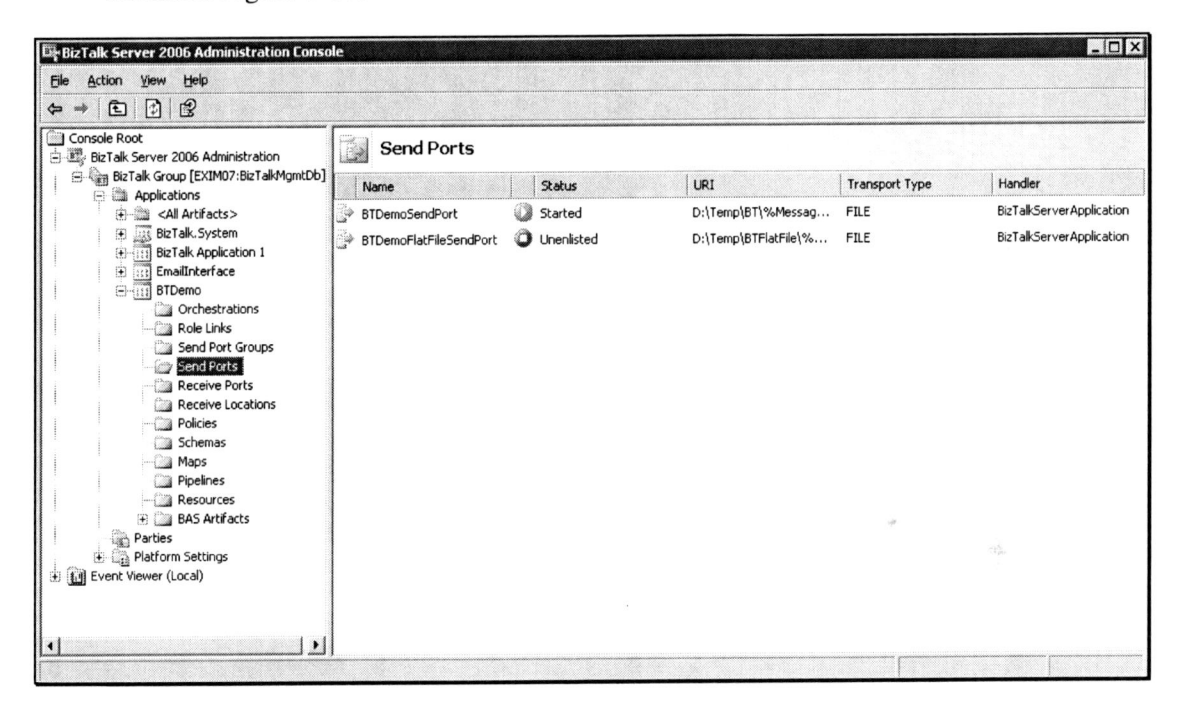

Figure 3-17. BTDemo send ports

6. Start the send port by right-clicking the BTDemo.FlatFileSendPort row and selecting the Start menu option.

Configure the Application

Configure the BTDemo application as follows:

1. Right-click the BTDemo node and selecting the Configure menu option. Your screen should resemble Figure 3-18.

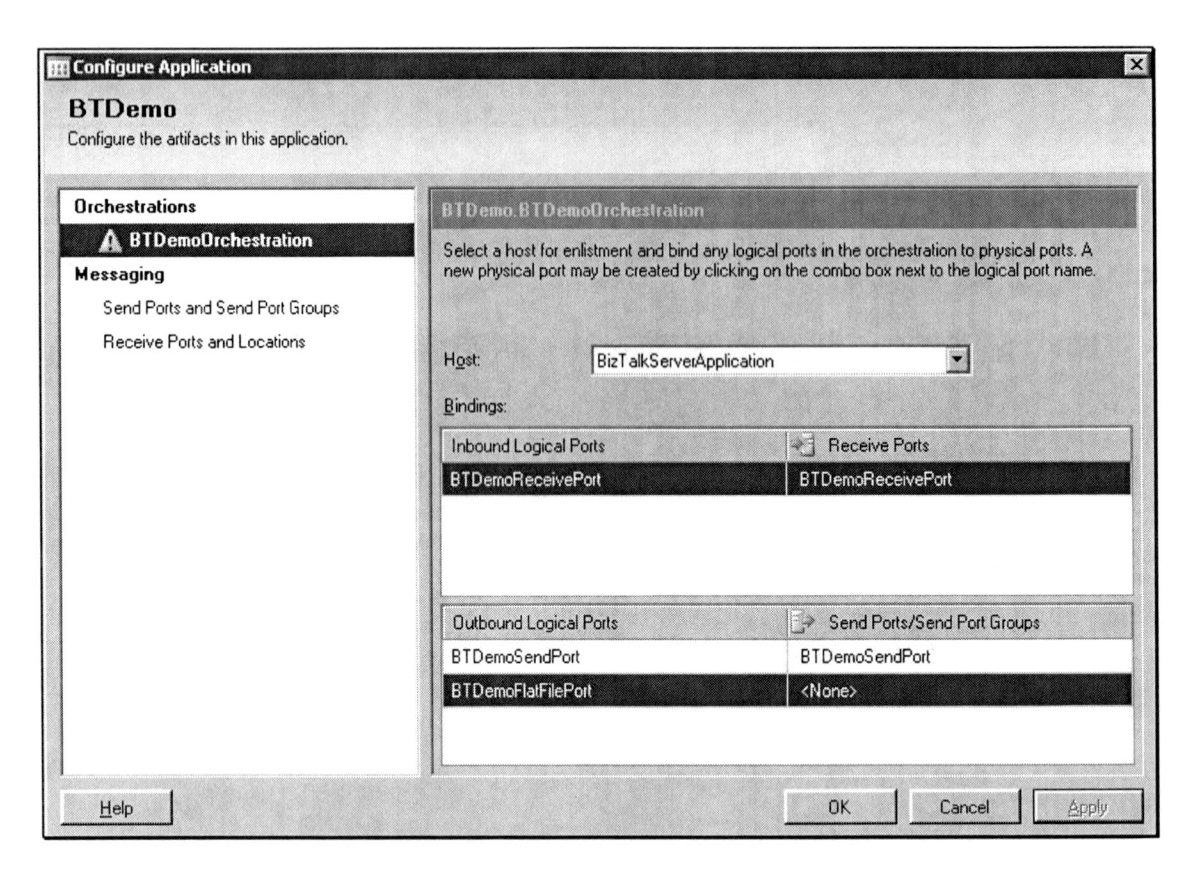

Figure 3-18. BTDemo application configuration

2. Assign a value to the Outbound Logical Ports ➤ BTDemoFlatFilePort property by selecting the Send Ports ➤ BTDemoFlatFilePort option. Your screen should now look like Figure 3-19.

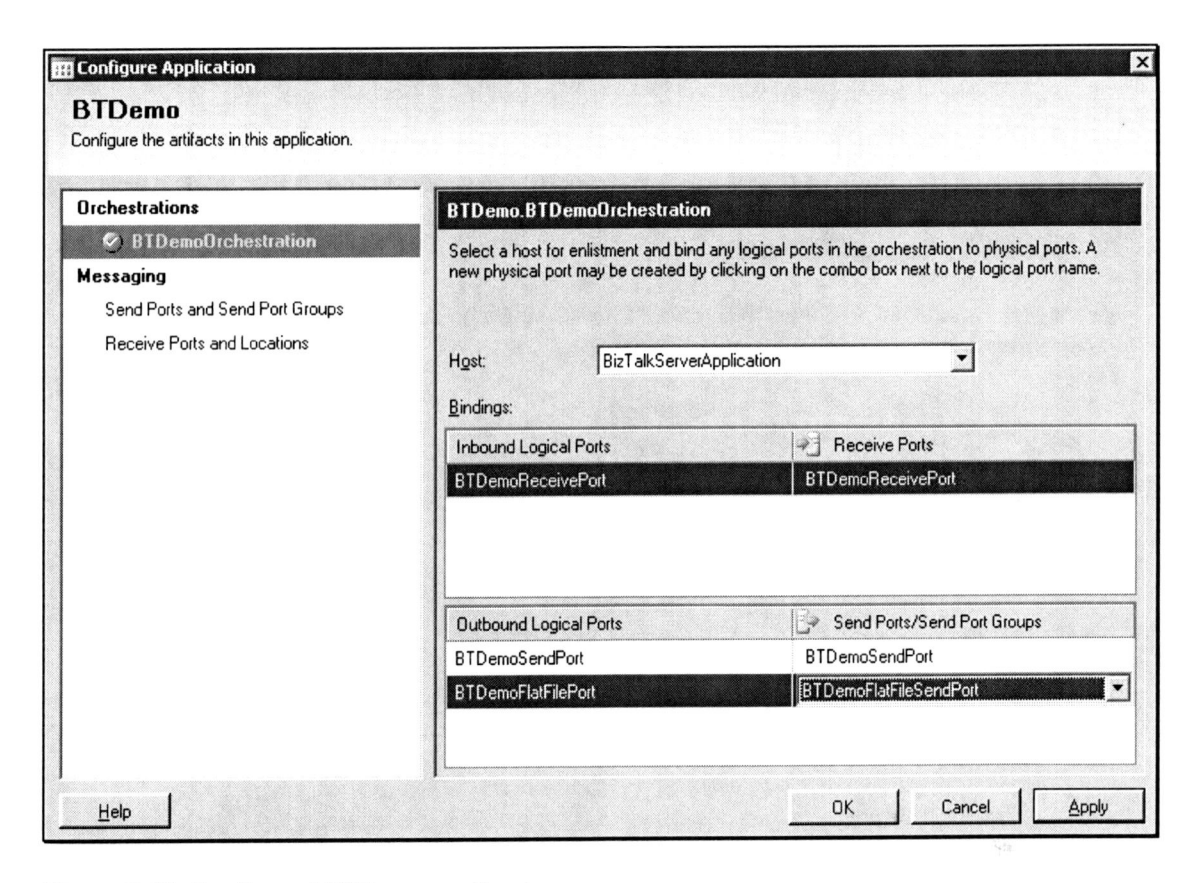

Figure 3-19. Configured BTDemo application

3. Click the OK button.

Launch and Test the Application

Stop and start the BTDemo application. To test the application, you will use the instance files that you used in Phase 2. To review the test procedure from Phase 2, you created a copy of the instance file generated when you created BTDemoEmailSchema and updated it so that its subject field was not blank. However, all of the fields in the original instance were blank. When you dropped the original instance file into the receive location, it generated an error message because the subject was blank. When you dropped the copy of the instance file into the receive location, it was copied to a new location.

Your test procedure for this phase will be as follows:

1. Drop the *copy* of the instance file created in Phase 2 into the receive location and verify that it has been copied to the location specified by BTDemo.BTDemoSendPort.

2. Make another copy of the original instance file and insert data in the fields *except* the subject field. When you are done, the contents of the second copy might resemble something like the following:

```
<ns0:emailservice xmlns:ns0="http://BTDemo.BTDemoEmailSchema">
 <transx command="command_0" datetime="datetime_1" />
 <send>
  <fromaddr>*** FromAddr Data ***</fromaddr>
  <toaddr>*** ToAddr Data ***</toaddr>
  <cc>*** CC Data ***</cc>
  <bcc>*** Bcc Data ***</bcc>
  <subject />
  <body>*** Body Data ***</body>
  <bodyformat>*** BodyFormat Data ***</bodyformat>
  <attachments>
   <attachment filename="filename_0" />
  </attachments>
 </send>
</ns0:emailservice>
```

Note ➡ The <subject> node should remain empty.

3. Drop the second copy into the receive location and verify that it has been copied to the location specified by BTDemo.BTDemoFlatFileSendPort.

4. Open the copied file. You will notice that the contents of the XML file have been copied to the new file and that its format has been changed from XML to flat file.

Sending E-mail from a BizTalk Orchestration

The BTDemo orchestration has been configured to write the flat file to a send port. Presently, the flat-file send port has been configured to write the file to a folder via the file adapter. However, BizTalk has other adapters that can be used (you already looked at the MSMQ adaptor in Phase 1) to process the file. The following example demonstrates how to configure the send port to use the SMTP adapter to send the contents of the file to an e-mail address.

If your BizTalk server is also set up as an SMTP server and/or is connected to an SMTP server, you can complete the following tasks. Otherwise, you can disregard these tasks.

Reconfigure the Send Port

Follow these steps to reconfigure the send port:

1. Stop the BTDemo application using the Partial Stop option.

2. Unenlist BTDemo.BTDemoFlatFileSendPort.

3. Reconfigure BTDemo.BTDemoFlatFileSendPort to use the SMTP transport, as shown in Figure 3-19.

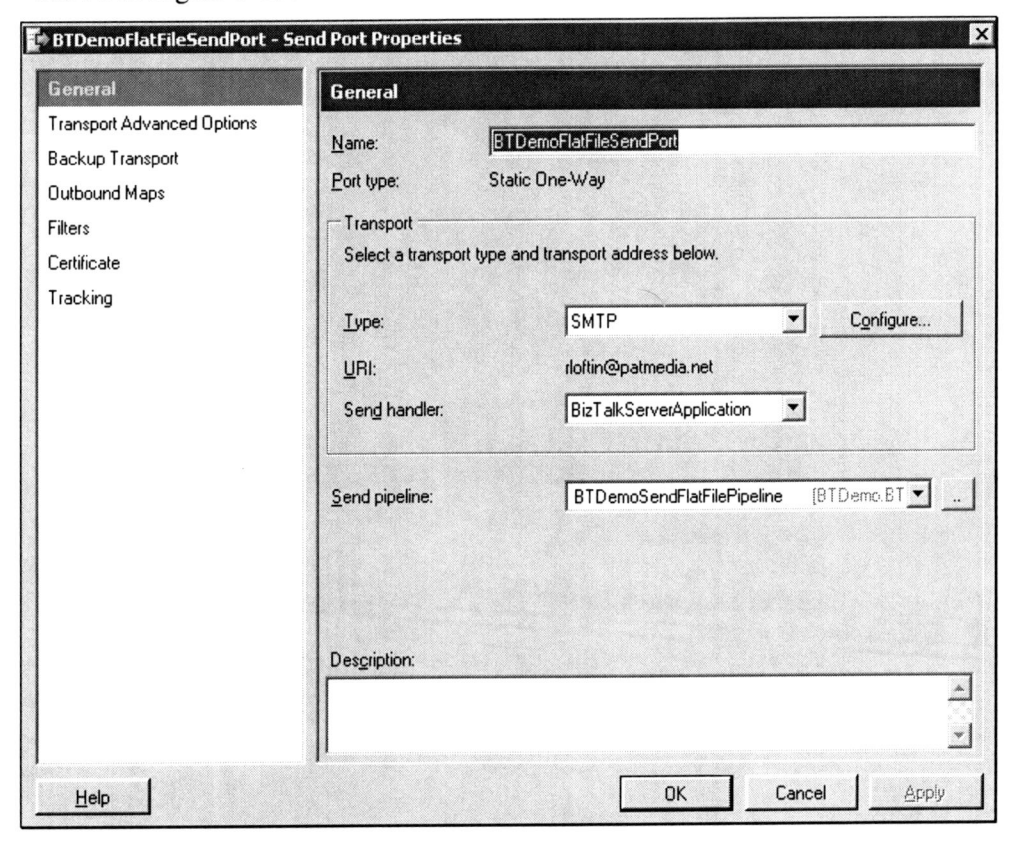

Figure 3-19. Configuring a send port to use the SMTP transport

4. Click the Configure button. Your screen should resemble Figure 3-20.

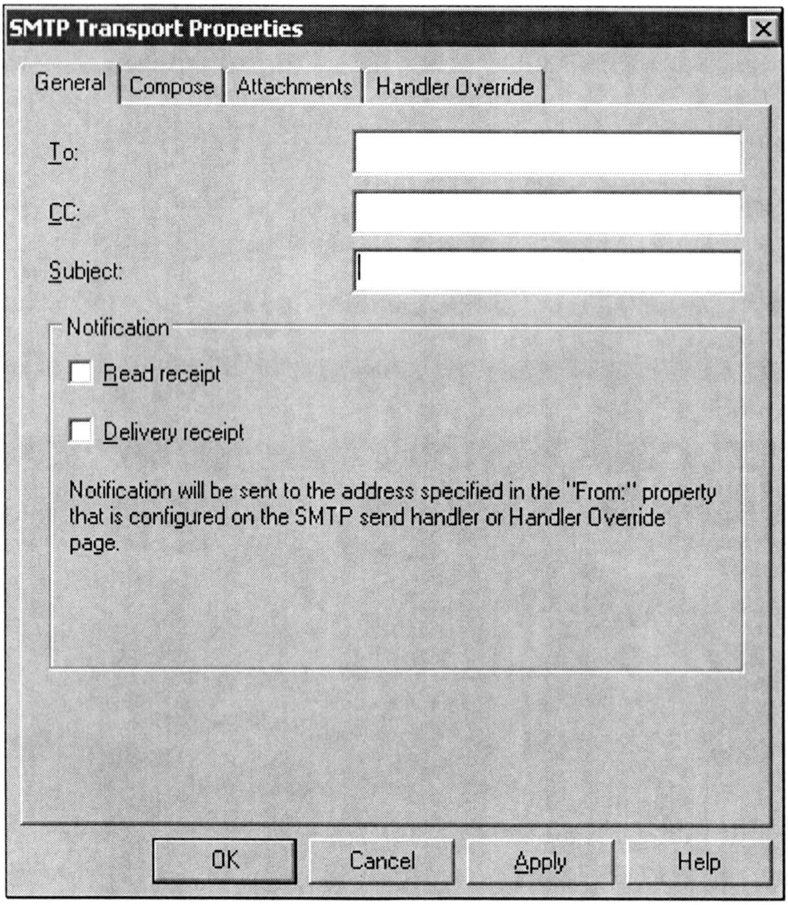

Figure 3-20. SMTP transport configuration

5. Fill out the information in the General tab (the To: and Subject: fields) and click the Apply button.

6. Click the Compose tab and confirm that the "BizTalk message body part" option is selected, as shown in Figure 3-21.

firstPress: Message Mapping 85

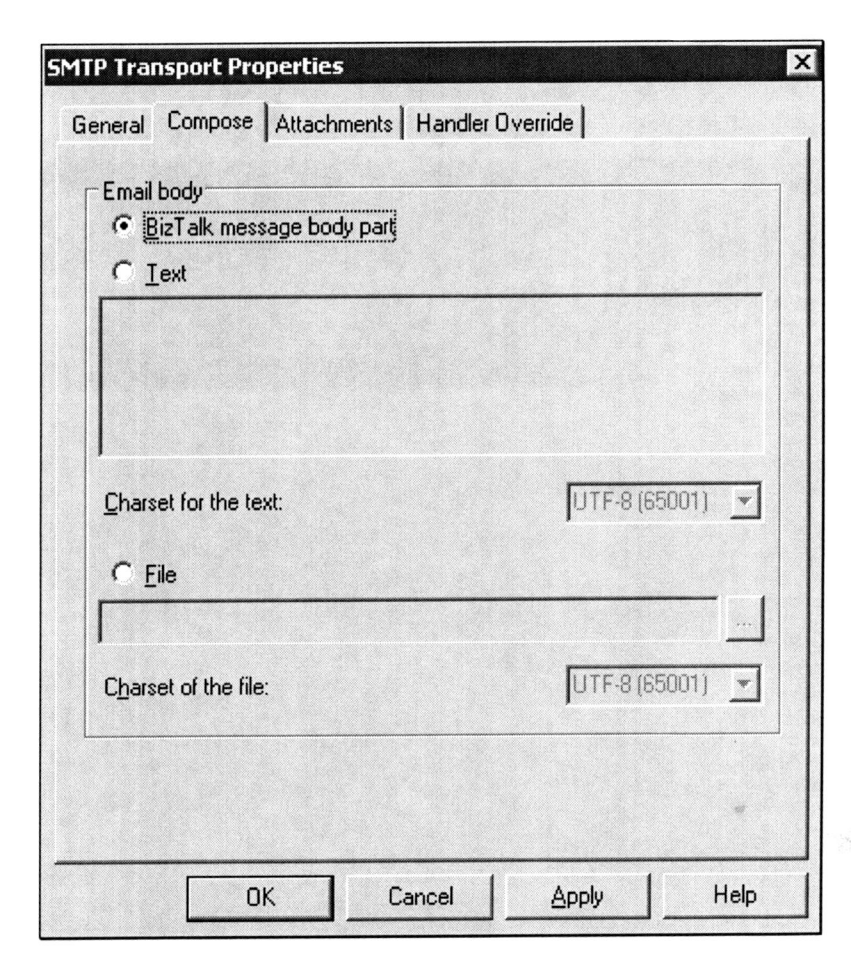

Figure 3-21. Confirming the setting of the BizTalk e-mail body

7. Click the OK button to close the SMTP Transport Properties dialog box.

8. Click the OK button to close the Send Port Properties dialog box.

Configure the SMTP Adapter

The SMTP adapter needs to be configured to specify which SMTP server should be used, as well as the e-mail address to use for all e-mail originating from the adapter.

1. Display the list of SMTP adapters on your BizTalk server by selecting the Platform Settings ➤ Adapters ➤ SMTP node in the left pane of the BizTalk Server Administration console. Your screen should look like Figure 3-22.

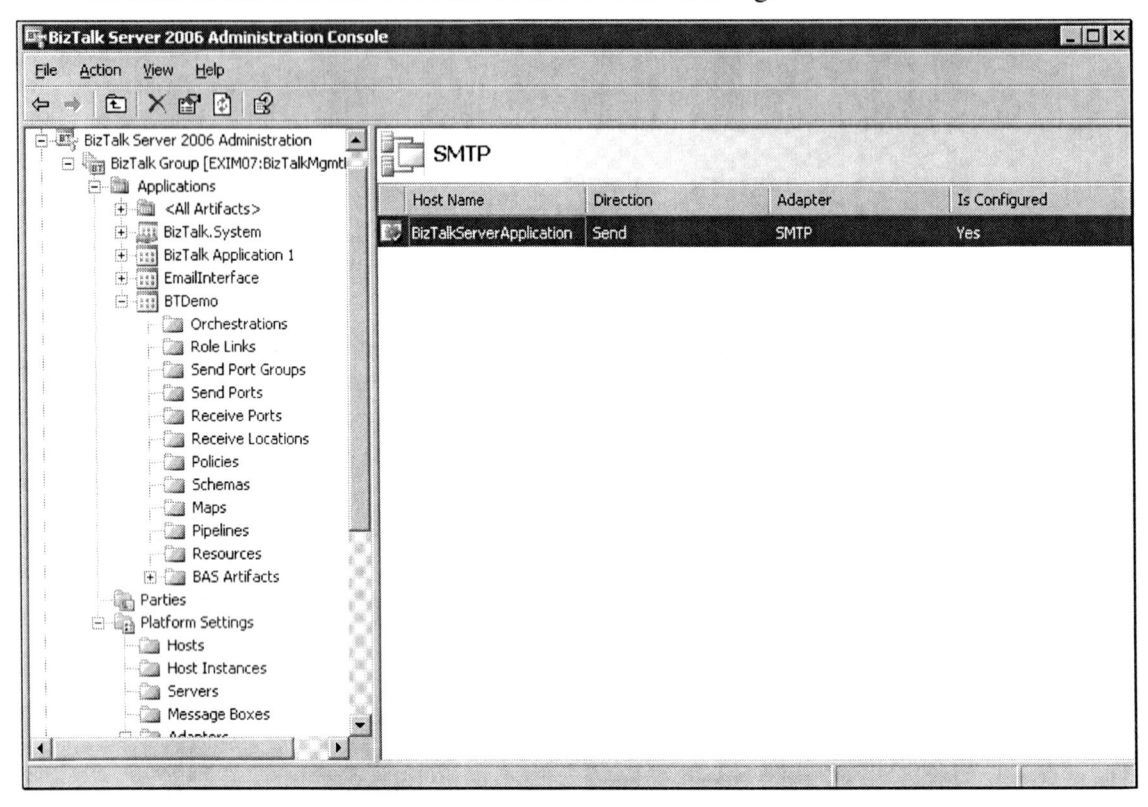

Figure 3-22. List of available SMTP adapters

2. Open the property page for BizTalkServerApplication. Your screen should resemble Figure 3-23.

firstPress: Message Mapping

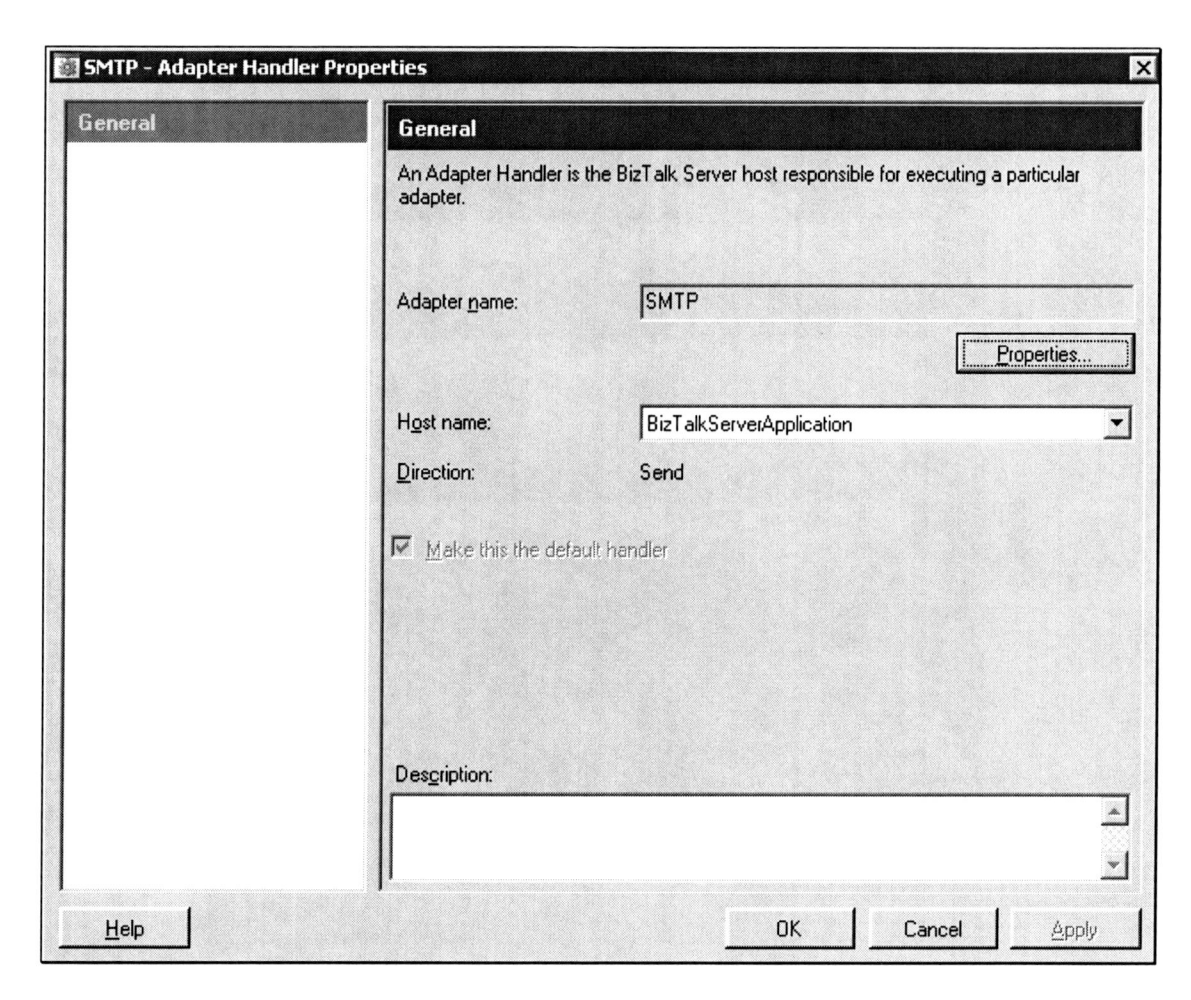

Figure 3-23. SMTP adapter configuration

3. Click the Properties button. Your screen should resemble Figure 3-24.

88 *firstPress: Message Mapping*

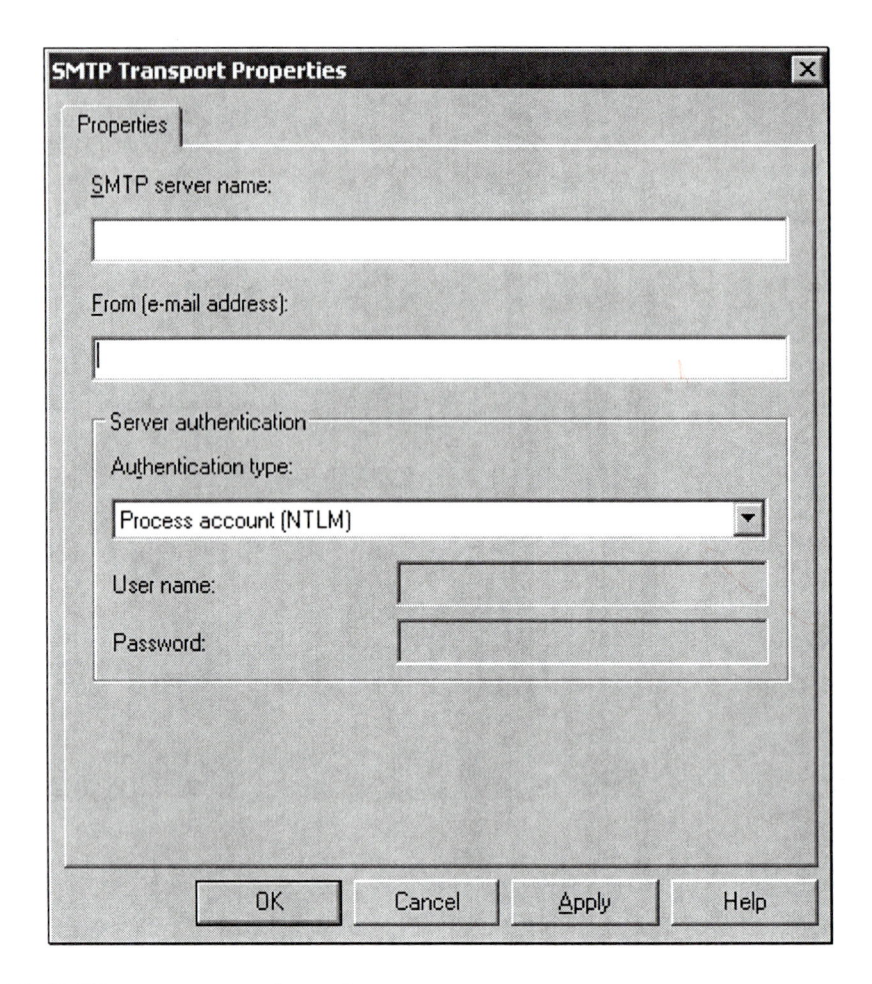

Figure 3-24. SMTP transport configuration

4. Enter the name of an SMTP server that you can use to send e-mail, as well as the e-mail address that should be used to identify the sender. Click the OK button to close the SMTP Transport Properties dialog box, and click OK a second time to close the SMTP Adapter Handler Properties dialog box.

5. Start the BTDemo application.

6. Refresh the BizTalk group.

Loftin

7. Restart the BizTalk Service BizTalk Group : BizTalkServerApplication Windows service.

8. Test the changes by dropping a file with a blank subject into the receive location. You should get an e-mail sent to the e-mail address specified by the SMTP transport configuration.

9. Bring the BTDemo application to a full stop.

10. Close the BizTalk Administration console.

Summary

Congratulations! You have completed your first BizTalk project. Although it was simple, it introduced you to some very important tools: Visual Studio 2005, the BizTalk Server Administration console, and the Health and Activity Tracking (HAT) tool.

Let's review what you learned in this phase:

- Flat-file schema files are used to define the structure and content of flat files. Even though the file being described may be in a flat-file format, the schema that describes it will always be in XML format.

- BizTalk map files are used to describe how data in messages is to be mapped from one format to a different format.

- By using instance files that match their BizTalk schemas, maps can be tested and validated at design time.

- Transform shapes are BizTalk graphical objects that are used to transform a message from one format to another.

Printed in the United States
201441BV00006B/1-10/P